A Chronicle of Letters

A CHRONICLE OF LETTERS

(Written to Various Newspapers from 1976 to 2013)

By

B. RAGHAVENDRA RAO

M.Sc. (Pure Maths), M.Sc. (Math Phys), Mil. Dip. (EDP)

Sr.(Life) Member: Computer Society of India

&

Former "Scientist" / DRDS

Himalaya Publishing House

MUMBAI • NEW DELHI • NAGPUR • BENGALURU • HYDERABAD • CHENNAI • PUNE • LUCKNOW • AHMEDABAD • ERNAKULAM • BHUBANESWAR • INDORE • KOLKATA • GUWAHATI

First Edition: 2014

Published by	:	Mrs. Meena Pandey for **Himalaya Publishing House Pvt. Ltd.,** "Ramdoot", Dr. Bhalerao Marg, Girgaon, **Mumbai - 400 004.** Phone: 022-23860170/23863863, Fax: 022-23877178 **E-mail: himpub@vsnl.com; Website: www.himpub.com**
Branch Offices	:	
New Delhi	:	"Pooja Apartments", 4-B, Murari Lal Street, Ansari Road, Darya Ganj, New Delhi - 110 002. Phone: 011-23270392, 23278631; Fax: 011-23256286
Nagpur	:	Kundanlal Chandak Industrial Estate, Ghat Road, Nagpur - 440 018. Phone: 0712-2738731, 3296733; Telefax: 0712-2721216
Bengaluru	:	No. 16/1 (Old 12/1), 1st Floor, Next to Hotel Highlands, Madhava Nagar, Race Course Road, Bengaluru - 560 001. Phone: 080-22286611, 22385461, 4113 8821, 22281541
Hyderabad	:	No. 3-4-184, Lingampally, Besides Raghavendra Swamy Matham, Kachiguda, Hyderabad - 500 027. Phone: 040-27560041, 27550139
Chennai	:	8/2 Madley 2nd street, T. Nagar, Chennai - 600 017. Mobile: 09320490962
Pune	:	First Floor, "Laksha" Apartment, No. 527, Mehunpura, Shaniwarpeth (Near Prabhat Theatre), Pune - 411 030. Phone: 020-24496323/24496333; Mobile: 09370579333
Lucknow	:	House No 731, Shekhupura Colony, Near B.D. Convent School, Aliganj, Lucknow - 226 022. Phone: 0522-4012353; Mobile: 09307501549
Ahmedabad	:	114, "SHAIL", 1st Floor, Opp. Madhu Sudan House, C.G. Road, Navrang Pura, Ahmedabad - 380 009. Phone: 079-26560126; Mobile: 09377088847
Ernakulam	:	39/176 (New No: 60/251) 1st Floor, Karikkamuri Road, Ernakulam, Kochi – 682011. Phone: 0484-2378012, 2378016; Mobile: 09387122121
Bhubaneswar	:	5 Station Square, Bhubaneswar - 751 001 (Odisha). Phone: 0674-2532129, Mobile: 09338746007
Indore	:	Kesardeep Avenue Extension, 73, Narayan Bagh, Flat No. 302, IIIrd Floor, Near Humpty Dumpty School, Indore - 452 007 (M.P.). Mobile: 09303399304
Kolkata	:	108/4, Beliaghata Main Road, Near ID Hospital, Opp. SBI Bank, Kolkata - 700 010, Phone: 033-32449649, Mobile: 7439040301
Guwahati	:	House No. 15, Behind Pragjyotish College, Near Sharma Printing Press, P.O. Bharalumukh, Guwahati - 781009, (Assam). Mobile: 09883055590, 08486355289, 7439040301
DTP by	:	Pravin Kharche.
Printed at	:	M/s. Aditya Offset Process (I) Pvt. Ltd., Hyderabad. On behalf of HPH.

DEDICATED
TO
MY (LATE) FATHER

(1895-1965)

BODDAPATI PURNA CHANDRA RAO
B.A., B.L., VAKIL
GUDIVADA (DIST. KRISHNA)

PREFACE

This book '**A Chronicle of Letters**' contains letters authored by me and published by various newspapers. They pertain to varied variegated topics of national and international affairs. They contain invaluable information on contemporary history and include general matters of significance. In fact, they provide an encyclopedia of general nature both educative and informative, even with respect to style of language. I believe the English reading public would find this work interesting and favour it.

I have great pleasure in appreciating The **Himalaya Publishing House Pvt. Ltd.**, for their unstinting cooperation and support given to me in bringing out this book under their aegis, in a beautiful form. I thank everybody of the Publishing house involved in this humble project. In particular, I profusely express my thanks to all Directors of the HPH Pvt. Ltd., Shri Harish C. Pant, and Shri P. Gopala Krishna Rao of HPH Pvt. Ltd., Hyderabad Branch for their untiring efforts in this context.

It is also my bounden duty to thank my dear brother Shri B. Srinivasa Rao., M.Sc., M.Tech. and Former Addl Director, Directorate of Electronics & Instrumentation, DRDS, New Delhi and now housed in Hyderabad, for his unwavering moral support given to me, while the process was still in the rudimentary stages.

I thank Mr. Suraj Prakash, PA, Directorate of Aeronautics for his kind cooperation in typing my letters, while I was in Delhi during 1970s and 1980s, and to Mr. T. Koteswara Rao of Satya Sai Graphics, Tanuku, subsequently.

My thanks are also due to my young friend Mr. D. Murali Krishna, B.Com., MBA and his able assistant Mr. K. Sai Shankar of R@inbownet, Tanuku for their kind cooperation in getting the print-outs and CDs of letters in the question.

Tanuku,

Date: 28-01-2014 **B. Raghavendra Rao**

CONTENTS

❖❖❖

1. ANDHRAS IN DELHI

This refers to your series of articles on various communities which have contributed to the richness of Delhi's political, social and cultural life. There was a no-table omission — that of the Telugu speaking people of Andhra Pradesh. Andhras have given the country two of its Presidents the late Dr. Sarvepalli Radhakrishnan and Mr. V.V. Giri. They have also enriched the culture of the nation by bringing to the national forum their famous Kuchipudi dance dramas.

Telugu is spoken by a large cross-section of the people of India and comes next only to Hindi. It is also called the "Italian of the East" in view of its inherent beauty, flexibility and felicity of expression. I was sorry that the Indian Express had not given, due place in its valuable columns to the Andhras and their rich cultural heritage.

❖❖❖

2. BRAIN DRAIN

The problem of brain drain has really assumed alarming proportions. This has been rightly highlighted in your editorial "Talent Wasted". Brain drain is unavoidable when the country of one's own origin does not provide suitable job opportunities commensurate with one's academic accomplishments and experience.

Research organizations in a country where qualified persons are mostly under-employed are a case in point. In general, a proper atmosphere for original thinking and research is lacking in these institutions. In addition, one is bogged down to a particular post for more than a decade for no fault of one's own. In these circumstances, it is but natural for one to explore other avenues out of sheer frustration.

❖❖❖

3. SELF-DECEPTION

Mr. S.A. Dange of the CPI deserves hearty congratulations for his condolence messages to both Mr. Fernandes and Mr. Namboodirjpad on their spectacular set-back at Chikmagalur. The Janata had moved heaven and earth to defeat Mrs. Gandhi. But, now they say that her election is of little or no consequence. They are patting their backs and sporting brave faces to suggest that nothing has happened. This is obviously an exercise in self-deception.

The electoral victory of Mrs. Gandhi may well prove to be a watershed in the present transitional period of Indian political scene. It is naive to brush it aside as inconsequential. There will be quite a lot of political churning. New alignments are bound to come indicative of the future political spectrum.

Her presence in Parliament may well prove corrective if only it can serve as a unifying force for the Janata coalition. They may yet give a good account of themselves before the next general elections, if they settle down to solve the country's multi-dimensional problems instead of harping on the so-called emergency excesses.

❖❖❖

4. POLITICAL VENDETTA

The punishment meted out to Mrs. Indira Gandhi by the Janata conglomerate by a majority vote in the Lok Sabha will go down in the annals of free India's parliamentary history as one of the most disgraceful acts. It smacks of political and personal vendetta. True, they have had their pound of flesh. But in the process, they have done incalculable harm to democratic values and norms. The self-styled democrats have at long last revealed their true colours.

The Janata may derive some psychic satisfaction that they have done what they could not do in Chikmagalur. But, this satisfaction is going to be short-lived as Mrs. Gandhi will in all probability, rise like a colossus from some constituency if not from the same constituency.

History is only a compendium of the stories of illustrious personalities. And, she is one of them. After all, she has ruled this ancient country of inherent contradictions with consummate skill which only a very few world leaders can claim. To think that she can be easily dispensed with is a myth and a wishful pastime.

It may be stated (with apologies to Abraham Lincoln) that the Janata dispensation is a government of the commissions, by the commissions and for the commissions. There is no hope and no deliverance for this country unless such a Government is changed soon. The sooner the better.

❖❖❖

5. KULAK BUDGET

The budget proposals of Mr. Charan Singh are atrocious. The plethora of taxes hit hard the middle income groups who are eking out a bare existence.

Slashing of duty on chemical fertilizers and diesel oil used in motor pumpsets will only help the rich farmers rather than the farmers of small land holdings, who have no monetary means of utilising mechanical inputs of agriculture, even if they so desire. Mr. Charan Singh may do whatever in his power to help the rich peasantry. He need not hit the citizenry below the belt to enrich the peasant population. After all, urban dwellers and villagers are not mutually exclusive but are wholly interdependent in almost every respect.

His taxation is of the order of ₹ 665 crores, perhaps the highest ever in free India. And pitifully, his budget shows a staggering deficit of ₹ 1,355 crores. The result would be a rise in the prices of all essential commodities. Fixed income groups would then, out of sheer necessity, press for a substantial rise in their salaries to make both ends meet. This again would result in further enhancement of prices. And, the vicious circle of price-increase and wage-increase continues unabated as before. All these point to further inflation and the economy going haywire.

❖❖❖

6. TEACHERS' PAY

The teachers of Delhi belonging to Government schools, Government aided schools, corporation schools, municipal committee schools and Adhyapak Parishad schools are on strike for quite some time now to ventilate their grievances.

They desire that the bill on hospital and educational institutions be withdrawn, as it abridges their legitimate interests. They are neither eligible for CGHS facilities nor are they provided medical reimbursement. Medical leave is only granted in case the sick join specified hospitals only, for their treatment. This is rather manifestly unjust.

They also desire that the disparity between the pay scales of Postgraduate teachers and principals, viz., ₹ 550-800 and ₹ 1100-1600 be reduced to the minimum. The selection grade of ₹ 675-1000 is given to the seniormost, whereas the teachers justifiably want that, after eight years of continuous service, everybody should be put in the selection grade. The Kothari Commission recommended that, after every five years, the pay scales should be suitably revised. This has not, however, been implemented so far. These are some of their demands.

These facilities should have been provided to them even without their asking. Unfortunately, the Government is in no mood to oblige them. This indifferent attitude of the Government is causing incalculable harm to the interests of the teachers and the taught as well.

❖❖❖

7. TALE OF TWO PMs

Two Prime Ministers have, in succession evaded facing Parliament and resigned. Mr. Morarji Desai, a self-styled moralist tried to stage a comeback through the back door. This attempt had been checkmated by the President by inviting Mr. Charan Singh to form the Government. Mr. Charan Singh too, has in his turn, followed the footsteps of his predecessor in resigning without seeking the vote of confidence in Parliament as ordained by the President. This is the tale of the two Prime Ministers full of sound and fury signifying nothing.

Sure of their defeat in Parliament, both these former Prime Ministers have acted in a manner which is against all Parliamentary practices and conventions. They have consciously tried to circumvent Parliament. It is a breach of Parliamentary privileges. Parliament has every right to censure these two men of straw.

❖❖❖

8. BLAMING THE PRESS

In your editorial, "The President of India", you have very correctly brought to the fore the not-so-charming relationship between the press and the politicians. It has become a habit with politicians, whenever they are caught on the wrong foot to accuse the press of misreporting. In some cases, they lament that their names have not seen the light of the day through the press, even though they are very close to the Prime Minister or some high dignitary in their tour. They want to see their names in print every now and then, though not in an unfavourable light. Instead of finding fault with the press for their own slips, the politicians should be careful in their speeches. It is very essential that there should be some norms or code of conduct and decency in dealing with the press.

❖❖❖

9. INCOMES

The Union Law Minister told Mr. P.N. Sukul in the Rajya Sabha that the Government does not propose to fix a ceiling or the income of lawyers. Subsequently, Union Minister of State for Finance informed the Lok Sabha that suggestions for wage including DA freeze are under consideration of the Government. These two statements read together substantiate and bring to the fore, in no uncertain terms, Government's ambivalence in curbing unaccounted money.

The Government is obviously too willing to penalise its employees, for its unwillingness and inability to mop up black money generated by private practitioners who include lawyers and doctors amongst others. But, even before thinking in terms of impounding the wages of its employees, it should first fix a ceiling on the income of lawyers and doctors. It should resort to reasonable taxation on the income, which go over and above the ceiling. The Government should also devise fair and legal means or eliciting information in respect of the incomes of all private practitioners as, in general, they do not reveal their actual incomes. This exercise will definitely yield good amount of money to the exchequer. And in the final analysis, the Government should desist from squeezing its employees by imposing wage-freeze on them, who are already financially hard-pressed due to sky-rocketing prices of all essential commodities.

❖❖❖

10. LIMITING JUSTICE

The Law Minister's statement in Rajya Sabha on 23 November regarding appeals in courts, is replete with ominous portent. He contemplated Government legislation to limit the number of appeals to one. so as to minimize arrears of cases in courts. He also stated that the delay in the disposal of cases is not entirely due to the existence of vacancies in the posts of judges.

This means that the malady is somewhere else. The Government should take all possible steps within its means rectify the lacunae responsible for the stock-piling of cases (without abridging or interfering with the judicial norms). It should also take immediate steps to fill in all the vacancies of judges' posts, which will enable the clearance of a part of the backlog, if not, the whole.

The imposition of restriction to a single appeal adversely affects the feuding parties. For in all probability, all the legal points may not have been covered in the very first appeal. And in such a case, a second appeal becomes absolutely necessary, in the interest of the concerned party.

The proposed legislation rules out this contingency and is a manifest negation of the very essence of natural justice and the true spirit of law. Further only those aggrieved parties, who are financially sound go in for an appeal, more so in respect of those involved in cases relating to property matters. And they are not worried about delays. Also, there are many a manipulative practice in courts which does not need description. As such it would be in the interest of justice and the public at large, if the Government desists from bringing forward such an unpopular legislation.

❖❖❖

11. ANDHRA PRADESH

This relates to your comment on Star Performance (15 April), which, is not factual. A separate Andhra State came into being on 01 October, 53 due to the fast unto death and consequent martyrdom of Potti Sri Ramulu at Madras in December 52. His fast was for an Andhra State with Madras, popularly known as Chennapatnam among Andhras. But, Madras was not included in Andhra, due to the greater pull of Tamil leaders with the Congress High Command. It is relevant to state here that Andhras were the forerunners for redrawing the map of India on "one language-one State" basis. Only subsequent to the formation of Andhra State, the States Reorganisation Commission (SRC) with Fazl Ali as its Chairman and H.N. Kunzru and K.M. Pankker as its members was constituted. Consequently, on the recommendations of SRC, States were carved out on linguistic basis on 01 November, 1956. Visaiandhra in the name of 'Andhra Pradesh' was also formed on the same date by the merger of Telangana region of the erstwhile princely State of Hyderabad in the already existent Andhra State, though SRC favoured a separate Telangana. Bellary was lost to Andhra due to SRC recommendations, Madras having been lost earlier. So, this was the real history.

❖❖❖

12. PROMOTIONS

This is to highlight certain lacunae in the promotion policy being followed in the Research and Development Wings of certain Central Ministries. Supposedly the brainchild of some odd and uncommon policy-makers a target date is fixed for consideration by the Assessment Board for promotion to the next higher grade. Only those who have completed a specified number of years by this target date would be called before the Board for interview to be held after the lapse of the target date. Usually, there is an interval of three-four months between the target date and the actual date of interview. Those candidates who would be completing the required number of years in this interval of three-four months to be eligible to face the Interview Board, will be left in the lurch. This is gross injustice. The target date and the interview date should be coincident. Otherwise many officers lose a valuable year in their service, by this indefensible policy presently being followed. This anomaly requires immediate rectification to save these officers from frustration.

❖❖❖

13. VARSITY MIGRATION

Press reports indicate that students of about seven colleges under Delhi University are on strike for more than a week, seeking redressal of their grievances and demands. Some of these demands relate to inter-college migration, adequate teaching staff, improved libraries, facilities for sports, non-implementation of proposed hike in hostel fees, hospital amenities and proper sanitation.

None of the demands seems unjustified. For example, the issue of inter-college migration could be considered sympathetically by the concerned college authorities. Genuine students who want to migrate because of lack of teaching facilities in a medium of their choice should be allowed to migrate. Otherwise, they will lose a full academic year, as they have no other choice except to withdraw from the college. Similarly, the case of providing adequate teaching staff should merit immediate attention of the governing councils of the concerned colleges. This is all the more necessary to maintain a reasonable teacher-student ratio. The other grievances should also be considered in the right spirit and a give-and-take atmosphere. It is hoped that the authorities will do the needful and end the strikes which will adversely affect the precious careers of students.

❖❖❖

14. ASSASSINATION AND AFTER

Indira Gandhi's assassination goes down as a dark chapter in the history of mankind. Nothing has so rudely shocked the conscience of the civilised world as this single savage act since the martyrdom of Mahatma Gandhi on 30 January, 1948. If the Mahatma died for Hindu-Muslim Unity, she died for the unity and integrity of the country. If the Mahatma gave the country its freedom and its flag, she gave it stability and strength.

The story of her life is an essay in courage and conviction, a saga of trials and tribulations and an epic of blood and battles. She was magnanimous in victory and courageous in adversity. She had her moments of ecstasy and anguish. Her finest hour was when she tilted the balance of power in the subcontinent with the formation of Bangladesh, consequent to the Indo-Pak war of December 1971.

Under the Janata rule, she was chased from pillar to post. But, she was at her best when pushed to the corner. She fought back like a wounded tigress and returned victoriously.

She was something of both Gandhi and Nehru. She had the dynamism of both. She possessed Gandhi's realism and cherished Nehru's secularism. She was made of sterner stuff. As long as she was on the scene, she fought the forces of disruption with unflinching determination. She lived like Nehru with grace and charm, and in the end died like Gandhi.

Dark forces of imperialism and communalism forced the partition of the country in 1947. Now, the very same forces are at work to destroy the country's unity and balkanise India. Indira Gandhi's foul murder is a pointer in this direction. It is time for all secular, democratic and Left-oriented forces to unite and combat religious fundamentalism to save India from dismemberment.

❖❖❖

15. MUSLIM WOMEN

Reference to your editorial 'Rethinking' needed. The necessary shock therapy has been rendered by Mr. Arif Mohammad Khan, by resigning from the Cabinet. He has upheld the democratic norms and secular character of our Constitution. He deserves approbation and acclamation of all secular-minded people.

The bill is communal in content and spirit and against the Directive Principles of State Policy of the Constitution which enunciates amongst other provisions that the State shall direct its policy towards securing for all citizens a uniform civil code throughout the country. These principles are not justiciable in a court of law. But this does not mean that the Government can enact bill so blatantly against the letter and spirit of the Constitutional provisions. It is a sell-out and surrender to communal and obscurantist forces.

One is reminded of Ramsay Macdonald, the Labour Prime Minister of Great Britain, who thrust his notorious communal award on India in 1932. It was intended to divide the people on religion, caste and even on sex basis. Mahatma Gandhi was, of course, able to undo the mischief of this award to some extent. Now, no Mahatma is available to us to restrain the Government.

❖❖❖

16. RESEARCH CLIMATE

There is certain 'Mediocrity' in Research. The malady is more than what meets the eye. The environment in the scientific laboratories, either government-controlled or otherwise, is not conducive to any serious research. This situation may be prevailing in some universities as well.

There is no gainsaying the fact that scientific research in India is plagued with nepotism and parochialism at all levels. Independence of judgement and innovation are not encouraged. No incentives are provided for really meritorious suggestions. Academic excellence is of no avail.

When it comes to promotions, less-qualified are given preeminence over others. This is due to the fact that promotions are wholly dependent on the ACRs and outstanding ACRs are awarded to people of normal IQ level, not for their outstanding work but for their outstanding 'chamchagiri'. People of real worth and who work hard get generally normal ACR with the result they get superseded. The cumulative effect of this situation can be guessed.

Scientific personnel at the junior level are mostly entrusted with routine work, and they are not expected to perform any kind of scientific work let alone scientific research. The so-called scientific laboratories and institutions are no better than government departments doing administrative work. Bossism is prevalent in these institutions stifling all initiatives.

Scientific research could gain momentum in India, if merit and academic achievements are the only consideration at entry level and thereafter in the matter of promotions. All the scientific laboratories and institutions should be reoriented, giving pride of place to merit and hard work instead of 'chamchagiri'. Otherwise, brain drain which the government laments about could not be controlled and there could be no hope and deliverance for scientific research in this country.

❖❖❖

17. SECULARISM DEFINED

The article by Prof. P.L. Rattan "Secularism and Religious Bigotry" (Patriot, November 14) was timely and thought-provoking. In Chambers Dictionary, secularism has been defined as the belief or view that the State, morals and education should be independent of religion and society's values and standards should not be influenced by religion. It implies that the State should distance itself from religious practices in the governance of the country.

But, in India, secularism is practiced as if it means equal respect for all religions. Not only this, the official media go out of their way to publicise festivals and functions of all religions with platonic fervour. Such an official attitude tends to promote religious bigotry.

The Preamble of the Constitution says that the people of India have resolved to constitute India into a sovereign, socialist, secular, democratic Republic. The founding fathers of our Constitution have thus visualised India as a secular State and not as a theocratic State. If we say we are secular, then there is no reason why we should be theocratic in practice. The Government should neither interfere in nor promote the religious practices of various communities living in India. In State functions, no religious practices should be followed. Only then, we can claim to be secular, otherwise, we run the risk of being called hypocrites.

Secularism is the very antithesis of the so-called religious fundamentalism. As such, one who professes and swears by secularism should neither appease nor compromise with religious fundamentalists. He has to carry on relentless fight with them to contain and curb religious bigotry.

India is, at present, at the crossroads of history. At this juncture, we should play the role assigned to us by history and prove faithful to ourselves. If we waver, then we fall a prey to religious fundamentalists and go down in history as boneless wonders!

❖❖❖

18. A SOUND SLAP

Your editorial "A Sound Slap" tried to dismantle the make-believe world of Congressmen. It is rightly said that the election campaign of Mr. Devi Lai was focused on the incompetence and malfeasance of the Rajiv Gandhi Government at the Centre. As it turned out, Haryana election results registered a runaway victory for the Lok Dal (B) and a disaster for the Congress (I). It became a referendum on Congress policies and leadership. Even in this hour of distress, it seems that Congressmen have not realised what would be the wages of immature and inexperienced leadership.

The Haryana voters have rejected the hereditary nature of leadership of political parties by the humiliating removal of Ajit Singh's Lok Dal *in toto*. This should be an eye-opener to the Congress which has almost institutionalised heredity in the election of its leaders from time to time. Even now, it is not too late for the Congress to realise the gravity of the developing situation and make amends to recover lost ground.

If a commoner makes mistakes, only his family suffers. But if a ruler makes mistakes, the whole country suffers. Mr. Rajiv Gandhi is no exception to this rule of nature. He is not made of "sterner stuff" as his great mother, Indira Gandhi was. Neither is he possessed of the vision, political wisdom and sagacity of his illustrious grandfather, Jawaharlal Nehru. He only knows how to be intemperate in language and how to behave in a cavalier manner.

❖❖❖

19. KARNARJUN

This refers to the letter "Karnarjun". There is a factual fallacy in the Mahabharata episode enumerated therein. It was true only to the extent that the serpent Ashwasen approached Karna, exhorting him to use him as an Asthra to kill Arjun in the war that was to take place subsequently between the Kauravas and Pandavas But, Karna, instead of turning away the serpent accepted its offer and kept it with him.

Karna did use the serpent as 'Nagasthra' against Arjun, in his two-day battle with him. Arjun looked bewildered as he saw the serpent racing against him. Lord Krishna who was his 'Ratha Sarathi' saved him using his might to sink the chariot a few feet deep into the earth. As a result, the serpent lost its aim and could throw away only Arjun's crown gifted to him by Lord Indra. As it was returning with pent-up rage in its renewed attempt to kill Arjun, Lord Krishna made Arjun remember 'Khandavadahanam' from where the serpent escaped. Where upon Arjun killed the serpent by an arrow released from his 'Gandeeva'. Thus, Karna's effort to kill Arjun with the serpent proved futile by divine grace.

The present political situation is not a contrast. It is similar to this episode. Vengeful attitude against opponents is not new to the people of this sub-continent. But, this is not to support Rajiv Gandhi and company in their strong-arm tactics to cowdown their political opponents. 'Facts are facts' and one has to face them squarely and boldly. Mr. V.P. Singh and his friends would do well to prepare themselves for an all-out war against the unscrupulous establishment and be ready to make supreme sacrifices, if need be, to espouse the cause they cherish if they possess a sense of history.

❖❖❖

20. THREAT TO SECULARISM

The criticism of Mr. Chandrasekhar's illogical views on the Kashmir issue in your editorial "Threat to Secularism" is well-timed. But the attempt to link the Kashmir issue and Indian secularism betrays historical evidence.

Secularism as practised in India since the days of Mahatma Gandhi smacks of hypocrisy. Secular Congress leaders Nehru and Patel accepted partition by conceding to Jinnah's theory that Hindus and Muslims are two nations. There cannot be an iota of doubt that partition of India has been a major blow to India's secularism. Still, we opted for secularism in what remained of India. Great. But again, free India's secular leadership always ditched nationalist and progressive Muslim leaders in favour of religious fanatics. Is this secularism?

❖❖❖

21. REUNIFICATION

Abdul Ghafoor's suggestion for reunification of countries in the Indian sub-continent has come not a day too soon. It is quite appropriate and refreshing that you editorial 'Covert aid to Kashmir ultras' reflected his opinion in the context of Kashmir problem. The idea is worth the consideration of all right-thinking people in the sub-continent. But, outright and hasty reunification would prove disastrous, given the prevailing turbulent conditions in the sub-continent.

Witness the strong centrifugal forces at work in both India and Pakistan threatening to rend asunder these countries. If India is saddled with divisive forces in Punjab and Kashmir, Pakistan is embroiled with divisive forces in most of its provinces. In Sindh, 'Jiye Sindh' movement is gaining momentum under the leadership of the octogenarian G.M. Syed with the ostensible aim of creating an independent 'Sindhu Desh'.

To contain these divisive forces and as a prelude to complete reunification at a subsequent stage, a loose Confederation of India, Pakistan, Bangladesh and Kashmir (incusive of PoK) and Sindh as well, if required, could be formed. There could be a provision that other countries of the region also could join the confederation, if they so desire. The federating units could, of their free will and volition, entrust the Centre or Federal Government with subjects like foreign affairs, defence and communications. If this arrangement works out smoothly over a specified period of years, then some more powers could be invested with the Federal Government by the federating units. It is time now to give serious thought to such a proposal and devise ways and means to implement the same in all its earnestness.

❖❖❖

22. A GOOD BUTCHER

The inevitable has happened. The dismissal of Mr. Devi Lal, even though belatedly, removed the main irritant from the Union Cabinet. He had not covered himself even with a semblance of glory during his tenure as deputy prime minister. It seems that, finally the forged letter fiasco had clinched the issue against him. Summoning all the courage at his disposal and taking all his National Front partners into confidence, Mr. V.P. Singh could at last hit the nail on the head.

A good prime minister must be a good butcher as well. Our Prime Minister should take courage to weed out all recalcitrant elements from the Cabinet to make it more cohesive and responsible than before. Only then, he can provide a good government to the country.

❖❖❖

23. PRESIDENT SHOULD ACT

Your editorial 'President Should Act' is a balanced comment on the political situation of the country. The Advani's rathyatra which created so much of tension in the country is basically aimed at vote-catching while the Ram Janmabhoomi issue is only a means to achieve that. Having realised that the National Front Government will not last for a full term due to incessant crises within the Janata Dal party, the BJP raised the Ram Janmabhoomi issue knowing fully well that no secular government can afford to accede to its demand. Mr. Advani, a shrewd politician, launched his yatra to develop contact with the electorate keeping in view the mid-term poll which is round the corner. The exercise ended in a fiasco with the arrest of Mr. Advani forcing the BJP to withdraw its support to the National Front government.

The successive pseudo-secular governments at the Centre had always ignored the interest of the majority of the population and did their best to appease the minorities to make sure of their vote bank. This has obviously hurt the feelings of Hindus. Mr. Advani, therefore, played the Hindu card to the maximum extent which would certainly help him and his party, in the forthcoming elections.

In the high-voltage drama enacted so far on the Ram Janmabhoomi issue, Mr. Mulayam Singh Yadav has emerged, perhaps, as the only champion of secularism by taking no nonsense from the fundamentalists, and upholding the secular character of our Constitution.

In these circumstances, President Venkatraman has quite a few choices. He may honour V.P. Singh's desire to test his strength on the floor of the House. In case Mr. Singh fails to get through, he might invite Mr. Gandhi, the leader of the single largest party in the House to form the government. Barring these, he may as well, call an outsider with proven political acumen to form a national government which perhaps is the only solution to avoid mid-term poll. The country can ill-afford another poll so soon in its present financial status.

❖❖❖

24. SHOWDOWN AT AYODHYA

Your editorial "Showdown at Ayodhya" seems to put the onus on Mr. V.P. Singh and is overtly sympathetic to the BJP and its shrewd president L.K. Advani.

The march of Mr. Advani from Somnath to Ayodhya with the holy purpose of constructing Lord Rama's temple on the ruins of Babri Masjid at Ayodhya led to communal tension in the northern states. It was the BJP which threw the challenge that it would withdraw its support if Mr. Advani was arrested during his rathyatra.

No government worth its salt would remain a silent spectator in the face of such a challenge which eventually leads to a communal holocaust in the country. The V.P. Singh Government faced it risking its own future in the process.

❖❖❖

25. UTOPIAN IDEA

Your editorial 'A Utopian Idea' is based on the premise that a snap poll would lead to the winning of a single party with required majority. But there is no plausible reason for such an optimism given the present conditions in the country.

With the communal tensions prevailing in the Hindi belt created by BJP President L.K. Advani to serve his party's-partisan interests, another poll would be a costly exercise putting an enormous strain on the country's exchequer.

The proposal of national government made by a seasoned and articulate Mr. Atal Bihari Vajpayee cannot be ruled out completely.

Particularly in the context, every MP irrespective of his/her party affiliations has to face the public seeking their mandate within a period of one year having done pretty little for them.

❖❖❖

26. FALL OF V.P. SINGH'S GOVERNMENT

Recent poll deal melodrama in Delhi proves that history repeats itself with platonic fervor. There is an intricate parallelism between the events that let down the nation in 1979 and 1990.

In the 1979, The Janata Government led by Mr. Morarji Desai fell in the wake of split in the party engineered by Mr. Charan Singh and Mr. Raj Narain. Subsequently, Mr. Charan Singh could realise his life-time ambition to become prime minister with the support of the Congress. But in no time, the Congress withdrew its support, with the result that Mr. Charan Singh made an exit.

Now Mr. Chandra Shekhar and Mr. Devi Lai became instrumental in splitting the Janata Dal. However, in all fairness, one must admit that the government led by Mr. V.P. Singh collapsed due to its own wrong policies, the withdrawal of BJP's support being the last straw. But Mr. Chandra Shekhar should prove his capabilities of governance soon so that he doesn't face the same fate as Mr. Charan Singh. History never forgives those who betray it.

❖❖❖

27. INDO-PAK TIES

Your analysis of the situation in Kashmir in your editorial "Unavailing third-round" is balanced. Any number of rounds of talks between India and Pakistan to normalise the situation would yield no positive results as long as the Kashmir problem is not resolved. The Kashmir issue is the bone of contention between the two countries and all other issues including nuclear proliferation are of secondary importance.

Legally speaking, the whole of Kashmir is a part of India, including the Pak-occupied Kashmir.

While negotiating with Pakistan over the issue, we should make our stand clear that Pakistan should stop training the militants of Kashmir and Punjab and all training camps in Pakistan should be closed forthwith. Pakistan aiding Kashmir and Punjab militants is an unfriendly act. Pakistan should prove its bonafides of friendship with India which it has not done so far. There can be no lasting peace in the sub-continent unless Pakistan wants it. No talks would be fruitful unless Pakistan proves its peaceful intentions by words and deeds.

❖❖❖

28. THE YES VOTE

The 'Yes' vote in favour of President De Klerk's reforms is significant more so, it happened despite staunch opposition by the hardcore conservative, Mr. Treumicht. It enables Mr. Klerk to implement the reform process he initiated to dismantle apartheid in South Africa.

As a preliminary step, he should immediately accept Mr. Nelson Mandela's proposal for the formation of an Interim government.

The South African all-Whites' referendum leaves many crucial questions unanswered. Are the whites ready to allow their Black brethren in their townships without confining them to the ghettos? Are they willing to give equal partnership to the Blacks in every walk of life?

The need of the hour is a social transformation. It is time both the Whites and Blacks shed their antipathy towards one another. They should merge on equal footing in every field, without racial discrimination. Only then the 'Yes' vote of the Whites would be meaningful.

In this context, it is appropriate to remember Mahatma Gandhi as he has been the first to denounce racial discrimination. He himself experienced brutal treatment from the Whites of South Africa, in the early part of this century.

Were he alive today, he would have been the happiest person to witness a visible change of heart in South Africa.

❖❖❖

29. REVISE PROPERTY TAX

Revision of property tax on the basis of plinth area to augment the incomes of civic bodies goes against the well-established principles of economics.

As is in vogue so far, assessment of property tax. Based on the rental value of property is governed by economic principles formulated by celebrated economists like Keynes and Ricardo. An extension of these principles reveals that rent is an interest collected by the house-owner from tenants. Its value is the sum-total of the rents obtained on a house by its owner. It is an income of the house-owner and hence taxable. It is quite similar to the income tax levied on interests earned by a person on fixed deposits and other investments.

If the Government now resorts to taxing the house-owner based on the plinth area of the house, it amounts to demanding a certain percentage or a share in the market value of the house, every half year. More so because, in a good number of cases in small towns, some houses may not yield sizeable incomes by way of rents, either being very old or having been in use by the owners themselves. In many cases, estimates have revealed that this new system of property tax if enforced would be 7 to 10 times that of the existing one. It is against all norms of economic justice.

If there are lacunae in the existing system of taxation, they should be rectified and improved upon. The tax may also be increased by about 20 to 30 per cent to fill in the coffers of the municipalities. Even before doing this, these civic bodies should be advised to curtail their own unproductive and wasteful expenditure. History teaches us that unimaginative and harsh measures would end up in a fiasco. When Mohmood Bin Tughlak imposed heavy taxation in the Gangetic plains to boost his exchequer, the tenants ran away from their fertile fields making them barren. Let this not happen in Andhra, in respect of house-owners.

The Government had done, well in postponing the levy of the new property tax till September this year. It would be well-advised to postpone the said tax sine die to honour the people's will.

❖❖❖

30. UNPOPULAR MOVE

The plinth-area-based property tax to be implemented by the Government from October 92 has been agitating the public mind for quite some time now. It is made out that the new taxation proposals have been evolved to check malpractices and under-assessment and to boost the incomes of the municipalities, ostensibly under the lofty premise of improving civic amenities. The rationale behind this unpopular move is not well understood.

Adopting plinth area as the basis for property tax is unheard of in economic theory of rent propounded by celebrated economists like Keynes and Ricardo. Rent is an interest collected by the house-owner by leasing a portion of his house to a tenant in need. The amount of rent is fixed by mutual consent, depending on demand and availability of accommodation in the particular area where the house is situated. It is an income of the house-owner and hence taxable. It is analogous to the income-tax levied on interests earned by a person on fixed deposits and other investments.

The Government proposes to tax the house-owner taking one square meter of plinth area as a unit for the evaluation of tax. It amounts to demanding a certain percentage or a share in the market value of the house. More so because, in a good number of cases, in small towns, some houses may not yield sizeable incomes by way of rents, either being very old or being used by the owners themselves. In many cases, the estimates have revealed that the new property tax would be 7 to 10 times that of the existing one.

In the case of pensioners, they invest their pensionary benefits mostly in building own houses and eke out a bare existence with the meagre pensions they get, as the cost of living increases. The new property tax imposes an unbearable burden on them, making their lives even more miserable.

It stands to reason that before implementing such a draconian measure, civic bodies should be advised to cut down their own unproductive and wasteful expenditure. A case study should be undertaken about the income and expenditure of each municipality and the civic amenities they have provided over a period of 10 years. If a case is still made out for enhancing the incomes of the municipalities, then the existing tax may be raised by about 10 per cent in the first instance. In the meantime, the Government should go in for a public opinion poll or even a referendum over the new taxation proposals. Public opinion must be respected as we say that ours is a Westminster type of liberal democracy as opposed to oligarchy or autocracy. Till then, implementation of the new tax system should be put in abeyance to respect the people's will.

❖❖❖

31. ANTI-ARRACK STIR

The women's movement against the production, sale and consumption of arrack, which began with a bang at Nellore, is gaining momentum day by day. It is a movement for saving their men, their families and society as a whole from ruin. It is indeed a sad comment on the Congress government that it has turned a Nelson's eye on the issue.

The anti-arrack crusade was part and parcel of the Congress culture and non-cooperation movement spearheaded by Mahatma Gandhi in the twenties and thirties of this century. In fact, it was one of the three principal planks of Gandhiji's constructive programme, the other two being khadi and elimination of untouchability. Accordingly, when the Congress took over the reins of power in 1937 in the Madras Presidency, under the Government of India Act, 1935, a ban on liquor consumption was imposed and implemented. It was done to honour Gandhiji's ideals and the party's commitment to the less privileged sections of society. The subsequent loss of income was made good by the levy of sales tax. However, the ban was circumvented and country liquor was made and sold in secrecy.

Prohibition was lifted in Andhra area in 1960 to bring it in uniformity with Telangana and thus boost the abkari income of the State as a whole. The Janata Government which came to power at the Centre in 1977 dealt with the problem in a novel manner by formulating and enacting a 12-point programme of prohibition, to be implemented throughout the length and breadth of the country. But prohibition being a state subject, its enforcement ran into rough weather. As a result, the sale of country liquor continued without let or hindrance in a number of states, including Andhra Pradesh.

Now, after a lapse of 15 years following the Janata government experiment, the women of Andhra Pradesh have realised the grave social injustice being perpetrated on them by a male-dominated society and took up cudgels against liquor production. They have brought about a new awakening in OBCs, SCs and STs. Their fight against liquor is both moral and social in sum and substance. It is an irony that this movement has the support of all sections of society and of major political parties with the exception of Congress.

The government's social welfare programmes are meaningless without effective prohibition. Before it becomes too late, the government would do well to impose prohibition once again.

❖❖❖

32. THE CONGRESS CULTURE

This has reference to your editorial, "Sticking to Bad Old Ways". It is rightly said that the Congress Party continues to operate in the same top-down fashion as it did under the Gandhi. From its inception in December, 1885 to the advent Mahatma Gandhi on the national scene, there used to be full-blooded democracy in Congress. Slowly but steadily, Gandhiji became the uncrowned monarch and his word was law for the Congressmen.

To go against the wishes of Gandhiji was the beginning of the end of the career of any Congress leader, whatever be his popularity-rating among the people. For instance, Subhash Chandra Bose became Congress president in 1936, against the wishes of Gandhiji, defeating Dr. B. Pattabhi Sitaramaiah whom the whole CWC supported. But eventually, Bose had to quit the post due to the non-cooperation of the CWC and Gandhiji. Subsequently, Bose left the party in anguish and disgust. Similarly, Tanguturi Prakasam, a leader in his own right, became the CM of Madras Presidency in 1946, again against the wishes of Gandhiji. And within 11 months he was removed from office.

In the Nehru era, Nehru was the High Command. Purushottam Das Tandon became the Congress president against the wishes of Nehru in the fifties. But ultimately he had to bow out of office, unable to pull on with Nehru. In the seventies, Mrs. Indira Gandhi became the great helmswoman of Congress and it was a child's play for her to remove and appoint CMs, just like pawns on a chess board. Nobody dared to stand up to her. Rajiv followed in the footsteps of his mother, though he was not as astute and shrewd as she was. All this goes to show that Congress has always been dependent on a single powerful leader. It was always imposition from above in Congress. Mr. P.V. Narasimha Rao acted only as he should have, making it appear that the incumbent CM is his nominee. His democratisation of Congress is only eyewash. Old habits die hard.

❖❖❖

33. OPPOSITION'S ROLE

This has reference to the editorial, 'Confrontationist Course'. It brings up the question of the rightful role of the Opposition in the Westminster type of parliamentary democracy like ours. A responsible opposition is a pre-requisite for the satisfactory functioning of a democratic parliament. The Opposition has to oppose, no doubt, since dissent is the essence of democracy. But it cannot and should not act on the premise that opposition is for opposition's sake. Its criticism of the government must be constructive. It should oppose the government whenever necessary and support it if the occasion demands.

The Opposition has more onerous duties than the treasury benches in a functioning democracy. It has to put the government always on tenterhooks for good governance. It should curb the government's tendency to ride roughshod over the people's rights and invest itself with unbridled powers. Acts of omission and commission of the government should be brought to the notice of the people. But primarily, it is through debate, discussion and consensus in Parliament that the Opposition and government have to evolve national policies and formulate legislation on all matters of public importance. It is the very anti-thesis of democracy that either the Opposition or the government should resort to the organization of an active participation in street demonstrations which sometimes turn violent. And street politics should be avoided at all costs. In this regard, our parliamentarians may take a leaf out of the book of British Parliament, the mother of all parliaments.

Viewed in this perspective, the conduct of all political parties including Congress does not seem to be above board. After May/June 1991 general elections, the BJP has been cast in the role of the principal opposition. So far, it has discharged its assigned role commendably well with caution and restraint. It is to its credit that, for the first time in free India's parliamentary history, it has shown how a responsible opposition should conduct itself in a democracy.

❖❖❖

34. SECULARISM, THE ONLY HOPE

Dr. Rafiq Zakaria's article, 'The weapon of hatred', makes a pathetic reading. It is written more out of anguish than in anger. In the concluding paragraph, he expresses his abiding faith in the ultimate success of Gandhian values. In fact, Gandhiji viewed Hindus and Muslims as the two eyes of India personified. If these eyes work at cross purposes, then the result would be chaos and allround darkness. This had happened in British India leading to the partition of the sub-continent and consequent communal violence on both sides of the divide. The same has happened again due to the heat and dust raised by Mr. Advani's rathyatras. The present situation in the country may well lead to the demolition of the secular foundation of the Indian state.

The twin words, state and secular, are mostly misinterpreted in the Indian context. State as a concept has no religion. Its business is to govern and govern firmly. Even so, it is not a police-state but a well-policed state. By definition, it is an organized political entity with a government recognized by the people. The word secular is a direct derivative from the conceptualization of state. It is concerned with worldly affairs and not with spiritual affairs which are in the domain of religion. The word itself is English and its origin and orientation is western. We have accepted good many things western in content and form. There is no reason why this particular word be given a different connotation. But, surprisingly enough, our own equivalent of Plato's Philosopher-King, Dr. Radhakrishnan, gave secular state a religious connotation. He opined that the essential unity of all religions is a political reality which, in essence gravitates to a secular state. This is a travesty of the western concept of secularism.

Successive Congress governments have practiced secularism as "equal respect for all religions" rendering the Indian state a multi-religious theocratic one. Only Nehru practiced the western notion of secularism, keeping himself away from religious practices. And there was religious peace in his times. Later on, the trend was reversed. It has become customary for government functionaries to take part in religious festivals and functions. They take oath of office by swearing-in on their respective religious beliefs. They appease one religion in preference to another, to keep their vote-banks intact and their positions safe. Discarding the western notion of secularism which distances the state from religion is the root cause of the chaos in which the country finds itself at present. And, Congress has to blame itself for this sorry state of affairs because it has ruled the country almost without interruption since Independence.

Capitalizing on the Congress brand of secularism, sadhus, sants and Mullahs have entered the political arena making things still more difficult. They began dictating terms and conditions to the government. They have the temerity to proclaim that they are above the law of the land. To cap it all, the recent Hindu Dharmacharya Sammelan held at Allahabad has drawn up a political agenda. Let these holy men who want to champion the Hindu cause remember that Hinduism is the most liberal and the most ancient religion. It is not founded by anybody in contrast with other religions. Even if all the Gods including Krishna and Rama are removed, still Hinduism exists. One can be an atheist and still be a Hindu. It includes both believers and non-believers. It accommodates and embraces all sorts of views and is secular by its very nature. And so, the holy men would do a great service to the country if they do not meddle in politics and distort the essence of Hinduism.

History reveals that only Muslim invaders and rulers demolished Hindu temples. The Muslim population is not involved in such reprehensible acts, at any point of time. In contrast, this is the first time that Hindus have involved themselves voluntarily to destroy a mosque, misguided by the sadhus and sants. Such an act of vandalism is a serious blot and blemish on the Hindu ethics of tolerance and non-violence.

Religion is a personal affair of each individual and let it not be mixed up with politics. Such an attempt will only divide the people and lead to further vivisection of the country. People should, therefore, rise to the occasion and force the sadhus, sants, mullahs, kazis and men of their ilk to perform religious duties and not to interfere with politics. The people should also elect to the various legislatures only people whose track record is secular in content and form. The country would be safe in the hands of only those rulers who keep the distance between politics and religion.

35. NOT A HASTY STEP

This has reference to the editorials, 'A blow to democracy' and need for a compromise'. A strong case is made out in favour of the BJP rally in New Delhi's Boat Club, scheduled for Feb 25. The Government's decision to ban the rally is seen as a serious infringement on the legitimate right of political parties to hold public demonstrations. But the arguments forwarded thereto, seemingly fail to carry conviction. The issue involves much more than it is conceived in the editorials.

For the first time in free India's parliamentary history, the BJP has catapulted itself as the official opposition in Parliament. Its leader in Parliament holds the cabinet rank. In all propriety, it should behave as a responsible opposition. It is mandatory for it to raise all issues of public interest on the floor of Parliament. It is in its own interest to employ democratic procedures before accusing the Government on the same score. If it fails in its attempts to be heard in Parliament, then only it may take recourse to other forms of protests including public demonstrations.

Over the years, Boat Club of Delhi has become the Hyde Park of London or the Madison Square of Washington. It is situated in the vicinity of Parliament House, in the area between Rafi Marg and India Gate. Political demonstrations are a common sight here. In this context, it is pertinent to note that the capital's experience of public rallies is none-too-savoury. Way back in 1966, the Sadhu Samaj rally held in Parliament Street opposite to Parliament House took a violent turn. Sadhus themselves indulged in arson and rampage. Normal routine of peace-loving office-goers and the citizens in general went out of gear. Again, Mahinder Singh Tikait's forays on the capital city are still fresh in public mind. He and his men used to camp in the

Boat Club lawns with their rations, for days together. They cooked in the open and carried out their daily chores in the spiraling lawns of Boat Club with gay abandon. The whole environment became suffocating. The beauty and charm of Rashtrapati Bhavan-India Gate complex is spoilt by periodic assemblages of political parties of various hues. The politicians may at least spare the capital of mammoth public meetings and demonstrations.

As regards the government's decision to ban the BJP rally, it has acted neither in haste nor in panic. The BJP and its allies have betrayed both the executive and the judiciary by violating their own solemn undertaking not to desecrate the sanctity of the disputed Masjid-Mandir structure in Ayodhya. The conduct of BJP and its Sangh Parivar allies leading to the demolition of Babri Masjid on Dec 6 was too provocative to allow it to hold yet another 'mela' in the capital itself. The aftermath of the Dec 6 events brought about an unprecedented holocaust in major cities of the country. Viewed in this perspective, there is no reason to believe that the Boat Club rally of BJP would not turn violent. The government is wise enough, at least now, to disallow the rally, and save the religious peace in the capital.

36. ESSENCE OF HINDUISM

I read with interest Mr. Parsa Venkateswara Rao Jr's article 'Another view of Hinduism' and Mr. Donepudi Venkayya's rejoinder. It seems that both of them have theorised on 'what should have been' rather than on 'what is being witnessed'. While expressing diametrically opposite views on the present-day sages and sants, the former has denigrated them while the latter has eulogised them in hyperbolic terms. But, the truth of the matter lies somewhere in between.

The letter points to the indulgence of Hindu society in allowing criticism of its high priests, as reflected in the article. But, it is because of this indulgence Hinduism has survived. Tolerance of diverse opinions is the touchstone of Hinduism. Hindu society is an open society which embraces all forms of opinion and dissent. It is this characteristic that makes it very different from all other religions.

Comments on the modern sages and sants even in derogatory terms have to be viewed in a spirit of accommodation. After all, not every one of them is a paragon of wisdom and a symbol of saintliness. They are only shadows of our ancient men of unimpeachable character and learning. It is hard to find a Viswamitra, a Veda Vyasa, a Bhisma, a Leela Suka or even a Rajarshi like Janaka among our modern saints. A majority of them are only ordinary men in saffron robes. There maybe a few who are endowed with genious and piety. That does not mean the whole lot is above board. Viewed in this perspective, taking exception to their being called semi-literate sounds hollow.

Running down the western educated intellectuals as pseudo-secular progressives is cynical indifference to their status. Ram Mohan Roy, Vivekananda, Tilak, Gandhi and Nehru are all western educated who enriched the Hindu ethos, each in his own way. They have understood the essence of Hindu philosophy of life and interpreted the Hindu thought in modern terminology. They stand as shining examples of all that is good and sublime in Hinduism.

Again, differing opinions have been expressed on the leadership of Hindu Society. But, there can be no two opinions on the primacy of 'Gruhasthashram' among the four ashrams of life. Even the Paramahamsa, Tureevateeta and Avadhoota types of sanyasins who are authorised to preach depend on the Gruhasth, for their sustenance. Gruhasthashram by its very nature provides both political and intellectual leadership to the community. The idea of sanyasin-leader is age-old like that of philosopher-king of Plato. It is only an idea yet to be achieved.

❖❖❖

37. VAJPAYEE'S OFFER

This is in response to the editorial 'A Significant Initiative'. Mr. Atal Behari Vajpayee is the most respected leader and may be considered a secular Hindu in the communal BJP. His plea for an out-of-court settlement of the Mandir-Masjid imbroglio deserves unqualified support from all the political parties.

Mr. Vajpayee's suggestion is apt and timely. Particularly so, since the Muslim intellectuals came out into the open recently in

Delhi, from their long self-imposed hibernation and exhorted their brethren to reject their present leadership which has led them to untold suffering.

Mr. Wahidudin Khan, Islamic scholar, has given shape to their positive attitude by proposing a three-point formula.

In the developing scenario, seemingly favourable, the Government would do well to accept Mr. Vajpayee's proposal in the larger interests of the country.

The government and the main opposition should eschew confrontation and work out a solution for peace.

❖❖❖

38. PAK ATROCITIES

This is in reference to the news item "Protect Minorities, Pak told". The UK House of Commons, cutting across party lines, passed a resolution exhorting the Pakistan government to ensure the protection of all its citizens, regardless of religious belief. It is a well considered reaction to the unwholesome and appalling treatment meted out in Pakistan to its minorities in general and Christians in particular.

The immediate cause that prompted this reaction is the death sentence awarded to a Pakistani Christian Gul Masih by a Pakistani court for blasphemy against the Prophet Mohammed.

Population-wise, Christians form the third largest community in India. They enjoy equal status along with the other communities of the country in accordance with the law of the land. But the same cannot be said of their compatriots in Pakistan. Their status is that of second class citizens, as is the case with the other minorities in Pakistan. In this context, the Indian parliament should muster courage and pass a resolution like that passed by House of Commons.

❖❖❖

39. DEATH OF PUBLIC LIFE

This is with reference to your editorial 'Death of Public Life'. It is pragmatic and well balanced. Your suggestion exhorting the Government to institute the office of an ombudsman to be appointed by the President on the advice of the Prime Minister, the Chief Justice of India and the leader of the opposition has come not a day too soon. This office will investigate the charges against persons in high offices including the Prime Minister. This suggestion is worth implementing.

Acceptance of funds by political parties and individuals from business houses to meet their election expenditure is not new in this country. In turn, business houses have their say and sway in all policy matters. No party is above board in this regard, as almost every party has tasted power at one time or other. For effective and impartial governance, the influence of business houses over political parties has to be curbed. This can only be done by state-funding of the elections. It curtails money-power as well as muscle-power, the twin evils haunting the elections. A legislation prohibiting acceptance of funds from business houses by political parties would go a long way to eradicate the malaise.

In a situation where an earring Prime Minister refuses to resign bowing to public opinion, the role President has to play, comes into limelight. The President should also have the power to dismiss an erring Prime Minister.

Moreover, to provide necessary legal equation between the President and the Prime Minister, certain balance has to be struck between the two offices. In this regard, we can take a leaf out of the book of US Constitution, wherein various checks and balances have been provided to strike a balance between the President, the Senate and the Chief Justice of the Supreme Court, so that nobody can override the other.

When all these necessary amendments are made in the constitution, the holders of the highest offices will think twice before committing any impropriety.

❖❖❖

40. AGE BAR ON LAW PRACTICE

This has reference to the news item 'Age limit for enrollment as Advocates'. BCI has debarred law graduates over 45 years of age from getting them enrolled as advocates in any bar association in the country. This is a retrograde step which adversely affects the legal profession itself.

There is no retirement age for advocates practicing law in courts, whether higher or lower. As such, it is beyond the comprehension of any logical person to appreciate the rationale behind imposing an age-limit for the entry of qualified law graduates into the profession. If there is an age-limit for entry, then there should be an age-limit for retirement also. In the absence of one, the other looks unjust.

BCI chairman avers that some unscrupulous elements improve their qualification and get themselves enrolled as advocates after their retirement. It is uncivil to call those who qualify in law as well, in addition to the academic qualifications they already possess, as unscrupulous persons. They are not improving their qualifications as such but only adding a professional degree to their qualifications. There is no age-limit for the pursuit and application of knowledge in any field, if one has the aptitude and ability to do so.

If some persons on retirement from government service choose to practise law, it is only to spend their available time in an useful manner. They certainly do not pose any threat to those lawyers who already distinguished themselves with a name and certain standing in their profession. It takes at least a decade, if not more, to become a reputed lawyer. No doubt, retired persons do possess invaluable experience in their respective fields. Even so, they cannot earn a name as a reputed lawyer overnight. Viewed in this perspective, they should be welcome members of the bar, as their rich experience in various fields will be an asset instead of being an impediment to the bar. Again, the BCI decision goes against the fundamental rights of the individual, viz., right to education and right to work. A person is allowed to enter and work in any profession of his choice and there is no bar in the Constitution over this aspect. The bar council is therefore ill-advised to put an age bar on law graduates if they opt to become members of the bar. It will be doing a great service to the legal profession, if it rescinds the ban.

❖❖❖

41. KASHMIR ROW OUR OWN CREATION?

This has reference to the Union Minister of State for Internal Security Rajesh Pilot's assertion that the Government is confident of bringing back normalcy in Jammu & Kashmir. One wishes that Kashmir valley gets rid of militancy soon. But, the action of the Government in relation to the militants does not testify to this optimism. Recent episode of Hazratbal is a typical case in point. Indeed, the Herculean efforts of the Indian Army in securing the surrender of the militants encamped in the Hazratbal shrine have come to nought. It is difficult to figure out the aim of the Government in releasing the captured militants in batches. May be the Government is unwittingly engaging our Army men and the Pakistan trained militants in a game of 'hide and seek'.

Our Government is hamstrung by its own lofty ideals and misplaced magnanmity in dealing with the Kashmir problem. Hard-won territorial gains of our armed forces during the three Indo-Pak wars over Kashmir have been handed over to Pakistan on a platter by our government for the sake of good neighbourly relations. Instead of reciprocating our liberal attitudes and good intentions, Pakistan chose to avenge its defeat in the three wars by hook or by crook, but could not do so. As a natural corollary, Pakistan engaged itself in low-intensity proxy war in Kashmir by aiding and abetting militancy in that State for over four years, till now.

It is not as if Kashmir became part of India, through the instrument of accession signed by Maharajah Hari Singh on 26 October, 1947. It was part and parcel of India's political and cultural ethos for many centuries of known history.

It was integrated into India during the first century AD, by Kanishka, the Kushan emperor. Great poet **Kalhana** who authored **'Raja Tarangini'** a brief history of the kings, who ruled Kashmir along with other parts of northern India, was a Kashmiri pandit. Over the ages, the contribution of Kashmiris to India's rich cultural heritage was immense. But, due to lack of foresightedness of free India's first Government under Pandit Nehru, Kashmir has become a bone of contention between India and Pakistan. Kashmir problem is thus our own creation.

As regards the area of Jammu & Kashmir under our control, it is imperative to abrogate Article 370 of our Constitution which confers special status on it, because it could be one of the many reasons that contributed to separatism and militancy in that State. Then, J&K should be split into three states, viz., Kashmir, Jammu and Ladakh. Kashmir Valley should be put under military rule till such time the militancy is brought under control. Further, as a policy, the government should encourage ex-servicemen to settle on our side of 'Line of Actual Control,' by offering them necessary incentives in both kind and cash. They will form the bulwark of defence against any Pakistani intrusions along the Line of Actual Control. Only a sustained policy of firmness pays dividends in our strained relations with our belligerent neighbour.

❖❖❖

42. HISTORIC, INSPIRING

It is indeed historic and inspiring that our Parliament passed a unanimous resolution on Kashmir. It reflects the national will and resolves to defend India's integrity and sovereignty. It also warns Pakistan to vacate the areas it occupied in Jammu & Kashmir. In this context, the editorial 'Ground rules of encounter' saying that the onus is now on the Government to implement and translate into practice the ground rules set out by the resolution was apt and timely.

The follow-up action of the Government should be to stamp out terrorism in the Kashmir valley. The most practical way of achieving this aim would be to put the valley under military rule. The State of J&K itself should be split into three regions, viz., Kashmir, Jammu and Ladakh and treated on par with the other states of Indian Union. In effect, Article 370 of the Constitution which could be one of the many factors that contributed to militancy in J&K should be abrogated.

Further, as a matter of policy, the Government should encourage ex-servicemen to settle on our side of the 'Line of Actual Control' (LAC) by providing them necessary incentives in both kind and cash. They will form the bulwark of defence against any Pakistani intrusion along the LAC.

As regards the completion of the 'unfinished agenda of partition' – thanks to former president of Pakistan Ghulam Ishaq Khan for coining the phrase – we should be equally interested in it, as is Pakistan. For, so long as we do not liberate the areas of J&K which are under the illegal occupation of Pakistan, the agenda of partition remains unfinished. The Government, therefore, should give priority to bring round the world opinion in our favour and mount international pressure on Pakistan to leave PoK. Only a sustained policy of firmness and tact towards Pakistan pays dividends and protects our national interests.

❖❖❖

43. HISTORIC RULING

This has reference to the news item in respect of Allahabad High Court verdict that lawyers have no right to strike. The court has stipulated a code of conduct for the lawyers within which they have to operate. It is correctly said that lawyers enjoy the status of a middlemen between the court and the litigant. As such, he has no right to expose the litigant to inordinate delay in representing his case in court making him suffer mental and physical agony in addition to loss of his hard-earned money, by resorting to strikes. A lawyer indulging in such an act is liable to be charged with professional misconduct.

The court has correctly observed that lawyers cannot indulge in lawlessness and violence because of the liberty allowed to them by the law. No doubt, this is a historic and landmark judgment, another niche to Allahabad High Court's impartiality in dealing with cases. Litigant public must be happy over this epoch-making judgment.

Indians still remember the Allahabad High Court judge Justice J.M.L. Sinha, who delivered the historic judgment unseating the then Prime Minister Indira Gandhi.

❖❖❖

44. MODERN LIBERALS OF DELHI

This has reference to the article "Priorities of Indian Liberals" by Parsa Venkateswara Rao, Jr. He highlighted the genocide being carried out in Rwanda by different warring tribes. It is a human tragedy of astronomical proportions. I do consider him as one of the liberal intellectuals who dared to bring to light the inhuman and wanton killings in Rwanda and appreciate his daring.

In the process, he has done a neat job of taking to task some of the New Delhi-based liberal intelligentsia. One cannot agree more with him. These liberals generally do belong to the middle and upper-middle class strata of New Delhi's population. He pointed out that "in the zeal to uphold noble causes, the liberals, it appears, seem to make a fetish of their beliefs".

True, it is because nobility is not bred but is a quality of the blood. To uphold human tragedies like the one in Rwanda, certain amount of daring is required. Herein comes the importance of belonging to a certain strata of human society. Delhi-based liberals do lack daring to arouse public opinion in favour of helping the beleaguered Rwandans with medical and food relief operations either by the government or philanthropic private organisations. They are willing to strike but not as willing to wound, to extract concessions from temporal authority.

Now that the Rwandans' human tragedy has come to the attention of the print media, it is hoped that all liberal intellectuals, wherever they are based and whatever be their profession, would raise their voices to build up public opinion and force an unresponsive government to play its part in the relief operations at Rwanda.

❖❖❖

45. GROUND REALITIES

This has reference to your editorial 'Familiar Bluster'. You have put the Kashmir problem, hanging fire since Independence, in its proper perspective. In essence and in effect, the hard-hitting Independence Day rhetorics of the Prime Ministers of both the countries are divorced from ground realities.

Turning a Nelson's eye to the fact that the five-year-old low-intensity war unleashed by Pakistan has seriously vitiated the Kashmiri peoples' psyche making a dent in India's secular fabric, is to make our own position vulnerable. It is a grievous wound that needs to be healed sooner than later bringing back the age-old secular way of life of the Kashmiris to the fore.

On the other side, Ms. Bhutto seems to be blissfully happy to harp on the so-called 'unfinished agenda of partition' now and then. In the process, she is rather unwittingly stirring a hornet's nest. Plebiscite or self-determination being made out by her as the cardinal principles of partition does not stand close scrutiny. These criteria could not find an allround application in the division of the sub-continent.

To recapitulate a few instances, Sindh went over to Pakistan by a majority vote in its provincial assembly while in the case of NWFP and Sylhet district of the then Assam province, it was plebiscite that saw them in the lap of Pakistan. Again, Punjab and Bengal were partitioned and village was taken as the unit for demarcating the Muslim majority areas for merger with Pakistan.

To say now that the principles of plebiscite or self-determination could be applied to Kashmir is to engage in a futile exercise of shadow-boxing. Even otherwise, in our part of J&K, peoples' will has been ascertained umpteen times through ballot whereas PoK truly remained an occupied area and a pocket-burrow of Pakistan without a single democratic election to its credit. This is the situation on the ground in-so-far as Pakistan's claims are concerned.

As regards the Shimla Accord, Pakistan has been singularly successful in burying it fathoms deep by observing it more in the breach than in observance. Even India is paying lip service to it, tending to make it holy cow. As long as Pakistan continues its intransigence, our exhortations for a peaceful solution of the Kashmir issue through bilateral talks will be of no avail.

Our policy planners have to take cognizance of the fact that Pakistan is bent on internationalising the issue, making self-determination its talking point. Keeping this in view of they should evolve a firm and broad policy framework to contain Pakistan's unmitigated appetite to annex Kashmir.

46. A STATESMAN HONOURED

This has reference to your editorial 'A Statesman Honoured'. One cannot agree more with you, when you say "Vajpayee is one of the diminishing tribe of Parliamentarians who put their heart and soul into their work."

His mastery of Hindi language makes him a compulsive speaker in that language. Indeed, he has very few equals in his oratorical skills in Hindi. He is easily comparable to Prof. Hiren Mukherjee in these attributes, though the latter's medium of speech is English.

Yes, Vajpayee is a statesman as distinct from a politician. It is said that a statesman is a sagacious and far-sighted person who looks beyond tomorrow and the day after and is not easily enthused by polemics and petty squabbles. But, a politician is verily the antithesis of a statesman. His priorities do not go beyond the compulsions of today. Viewed in this perspective, Vajpayee's parliamentary career spanning over a period of three decades and odd makes him undoubtedly a statesman par excellence. And it is no great wonder as he is a liberal bred in the Nehruvian mould. The award of best parliamentarian is really a fitting tribute to his illustrious career as a liberal statesman and has come not a day too soon.

❖❖❖

47. MAKE THE BOMB

The recent forthright and unambiguous declaration of the former prime minister of Pakistan, Nawaz Shariff reveals only what the world knows too well that his country possesses a nuclear bomb and will use it against India in case of a conflict over Kashmir. This is proof enough of Pakistan's nuclear weapons' programme, if proof is required for those doubting Thomases in India.

Apologists for Pakistan in India over-emphasize the internal compulsions of Pakistani politicians as regards their belligerent attitude towards India on the Kashmir question. They tend to give the benefit of the doubt to Pakistan and conveniently overlook the inherent dangers of soft-peddling on its nuclear capabilities.

One is reminded of the retired General Sunderjee's book 'Blind Men of Hindustan', where he has unequivocally criticised the Indian politicians for their myopic view of Pakistan's nuclear perceptions. They are living in a world of make-believe and, in the process, are laying bare our armed forces to a nuclear attack. It is too well known that the deterrent to a nuclear weapon could only be another nuclear weapon. No conventional weapon, whatever be its killing capacity, could match a nuclear weapon. In the circumstances, Pakistan's nuclear threat can only be countered and thwarted by our own production of a nuclear arsenal with delivery systems.

Indian history is replete with numerous irrefutable proofs and evidence that India has always lost crucial battles due to its inferior arms in comparison with those of the invaders. We will be putting our national interest in jeopardy if we do not learn our lessons from history and go on harping blissfully on our exercise of nuclear option. This option has already been exhausted in the face of Pakistan's clandestine nuclear weapons programme and its possession of a nuclear bomb.

The Indian Government would do well even at this late hour to recognise the hard realities of the developing nuclear scenario in the sub-continent. The only option left for it is to rectify the nuclear imbalance.

❖❖❖

48. A LESSON FROM IRA

This has reference to your editorial 'Rebuff to Terrorism'. Your observation that the IRA ceasefire declaration marks a triumph of moderation both among the majority Protestants of Northern Ireland and its Catholic minority is quite appropriate and pertinent.

This denouement of eschewing violence by IRA, though very significant *prima facie*, could be more or less, due to the diminishing monetary returns from their Irish-American compatriots. Even so, it is a good gesture on IRA's part for accelerating the process of reconciliation between the Irish Republic and Britain.

It will be educative to go into the genesis of the problem of militancy and its origin in Northern Ireland, known previously as Ulster. This province of Ireland had been the bone of contention between the Irish Republic and Britain, since independence dawned on Ireland. The partition of Ulster from Ireland and its merger with Britain, on the plea that it had a Protestant majority, has not been taken very kindly by the Irish nationalists, including "Eamon de Valera," who subsequently became the first president of the Irish Republic. Sinn Fein, the Irish nationalist party founded by "Eamon de Valera" for achieving political freedom, was naturally in the forefront of the agitation for the merger of Ulster with the republic. IRA, the front-line militant organization of Sinn Fein had been fighting for this cause for over 25 years with little success. May be the cause is noble but means are ignorable. In the process, as it always happens, many innocents were ruthlessly mowed down.

Viewed in this perspective, the statement of Sinn Fein leader Gerry Adams that "a guerilla ceasefire could be close enough" acquires potential political significance. One can only hope that, with political maturity, sagacity and wisdom, both the Irish Republic and Britain could evolve a mutually satisfactory solution to the nagging problem. Such a solution should in turn, pacify the pent-up feelings of IRA.

Now it is for the militant groups in India to take a leaf out of the book of IRA and decide what is good for the cause they hold so dear to their hearts. They should realize that wanton killings would be of no avail to achieve their goals. They should give farewell to arms and demand butter for guns from the powers that be. They should work out a negotiated settlement of all their outstanding problems with the government and provide much-needed peace to the country.

49. HELP FREE PoK

This has reference to the news item 'Vajpayee's Call to Back Stir in PoK'. He suggested two very sensible policies for possible implementation by the Indian Government. The first one is declaring moral as well as political support for the liberation of Pak-occupied Kashmir (PoK) from the clutches of Pakistan. In the second one, he chided the Indian Government for not taking up the issue of human rights violations in PoK at the international forums effectively.

On both counts, he is on firm ground. As regards moral and political support to liberate PoK, it should be combined with material support. Otherwise, it means nothing. In the armed forces parlance, the best defence is offense operation. So far, we are on the defensive on Kashmir. It is time that we take meaningful steps to implement our Prime Minister's own assertion on Independence Day that the only issue left is the liberation of PoK from Pakistan's occupation.

As regards human rights violations in PoK, it is a matter which should be taken up by the Indian Government in right earnest in all international forums, if only to highlight and prove that Pakistan's human rights record is bad and it cannot point out an accusing finger at India on this score. Last but not the least, if the Indian government really means business in dealing with Pakistani intransigence, it should take up the human rights violations not only in PoK but also in Sindh. Sindh is the worst sufferer where human rights are trampled upon with impunity. The Indian Government should at least now react to the situation prevailing in the sub-continent. Else, it will be putting in jeopardy the security concerns of India.

❖❖❖

50. BILL CLINTON'S DIPLOMACY

The accord reached by the US with Haiti's military junta is refreshing and welcome. The junta has agreed to step down by October 15, thus facilitating takeover by the ousted but elected President Aristide of the island-nation. This is a laudable achievement on any count by the former US president Jimmy Carter. It is a tribute to his persuasive diplomacy. But it is also true that his diplomatic skill has been aided and abetted by President Clinton's brinkmanship.

Earlier also, in June, this year, such a method of coupling diplomacy with brinkmanship had paid off when a defiant North Korea agreed to allow inspection of its nuclear weapons' programme, thanks again to Carter's persuasive tact.

In this context, the US Secretary of State, Mr. Warren Christopher's remarks that this was one instance where power served diplomacy in an absolutely classic way assumes much significance. It gives an insight into the foreign policy parametres and perceptions of the Clinton Administration. One wonders if the Clinton Administration is following Bismarck's principle that war is an extension of diplomacy.

❖❖❖

51. AURANGZEB'S LEGACY

This has reference to Mr. A.K. Chatterjee's article "Malkani's Doctoring History". He has made a critical and incisive assessment of Malkani's article "Legacy of Hate". In the process, he has epitomized the so-called distortions of history, said to have been doctored by Malkani in his article. Facts are facts and one has to accept them. There could, of course, be no two opinions on the historical fact that Islam was spread by the brute force of sword and not, in any case by persuasive precepts and teachings of the Quran.

That being the case, in the beginning of Muslim invasions of India during 7th century AD, it was true that battles were fought by purely invading Muslim armies and purely defending Hindu armies. But, by the time of Mughal invasion of India in 1526 AD by Jahiruddin Muhammed Babur, it was altogether a different story. The defending armies consisted of both Hindus and Muslims, though the latter could be in small proportion. Such a composite defending army could be possible, since, by that time, the Hindus had converted to Islam or otherwise foreigners like Arabs and Afghans, have made India their home. Viewed in this perspective, Malkani's assertion that there were no wholly Muslim and Hindu army in India after Muhammad Ghori's advent stands to reason.

Mr. Chatterjee asserts that Hindu-Muslim divide is not "The gift of the British". This is far from the facts and truth. The Hindu-Muslim unity forged by Jalaluddin Muhammad Akbar during his reign continued during the reigns of Jehangir and Shahjehan for well over a hundred years. This unity so assiduously built up by these statesmen-like and wise emperors had, no doubt, been shattered by Aurangzeb. In his communal frenzy, he might have ordered the mass destruction of Hindu temples. But, if his staff had faithfully implemented his orders, then Lord Jagannath's temple at Puri and numerous temples in Tamil Nadu would have been destroyed, if one remembers that the whole India, including Tamil Nadu up to the river Kaveri, was under his occupation and effective control. History should forgive such a maniac personified by Aurangzeb. He was only an aberration in the long history of India. And, the West Bengal government cannot be faulted if it had omitted the unsavoury episode of mass destruction order by Aurangzeb in the history texts, because past history could not be used to sully and spoil the present and future.

In spite of Aurangzeb and everything else that contribute to division, Hindus and Muslims became united and fought side by side in 1857, in their unsuccessful attempt to throw the British out of India. Having learnt their lesson from the upheaval of 1857, the British realised that they could not perpetuate their rule over India if Hindus and Muslims stood united. So, they formulated their famous (or infamous) "divide-and-rule policy" which culminated in the partition of India in 1947. These facts disprove Mr. Chatterjee's assertion that Hindu-Muslim division had already existed, even before the British occupation of India.

Mr. Malkani may not be justified in his assessment of historical facts here and there. But there can be no doubt about his sincerity of purpose in doctoring history.

❖❖❖

52. IN REVERSE GEAR

This has reference to the news item 'Vajpayee Faults Reservation Criteria' (IE, September 8). He took a very wise, statesman-like and sensible stand in boldly emphasizing that accident of birth cannot become a criterion for denying education to any class of people. He elaborated his stand by saying that students belonging to advanced classes cannot be denied admission in institutions of higher education, just because 50 per cent of the seats have already been reserved for BCs, SCs and STs. It is indeed refreshing and scintillating that a person of his stature should speak against the discrimination meted out to students of advanced classes of society. However, his suggestion to open new colleges to accommodate advanced class students does not wash, as 50 per cent reservation would be made applicable to these colleges also.

If a student was born into so-called forward class or caste of the society then, it is after all, not his fault. To penalize and victimize him for a fault for which he is no more responsible than his parents is neither ethical nor legal. It is outright discrimination of the forward class students as against those of the backward classes. It is also in contravention of one of the fundamental rights of citizens, viz., right to education, enshrined in our Constitution.

Nowadays, there is an unseemly haste to call oneself backward, as it entails availing reservation liberally granted by the government. The 50 per cent reservation norm stipulated by the Supreme Court is being circumvented by the government in all possible ways. And thus merit will suffer.

Some sections of society which have seen an economic boom over the years since Independence are pressuring the government and it is buckling under pressure, so much so that there is every chance of the entire society being termed as backward. There is obviously no wisdom in this drift towards backwardness.

❖❖❖

53. GERMAN ROPEWALK

This has reference to your editorial 'Kohlossal Germany'. The coinage and construction of the adjective 'Kohlossal' from the proper nown 'Kohl' is at once imaginative, innovative and interesting. The victory of the German Chancellor, Mr. Helmut Kohl, elected for a fourth term, is indeed a tribute to his colossal (or Kohlossal?) brain, brawn and political sagacity. His outstanding achievement is the peaceful merger of the Communist East Germany with his own capitalist West Germany under his famous dictum "unity without blood, war or tears". He stands unenviable in contrast with yet another Great German Otto Van Bismarck, who, as the celebrated Chancellor of "King Frederick, the Great" of Prussia, forged the unification of over 300 and odd German-speaking states into a single German nation in the 19th century, by the judicious use of "war as an extension of diplomacy".

Though, emerged successful at the husting, Kohl's victory margin of 341 seats to the Opposition's 331 seats in the 'Bundestag' gives him too little comfort to embark upon any major political adventure. His passionate dream of a European nation-state is too farfetched to accomplish, simply because no single nation in Europe would be willing to sacrifice its own national identity. Great Britain is a case in point, where the Maastricht Treaty for economic and political union of Europe is facing rough weather. The echoes of their pre-eminence and supremacy of the past in almost all areas of temporal domain haunts even the Germans, making it too difficult to submerge themselves in a Union of European States. This mind-set of Germans makes it all the more difficult for Mr. Kohl to achieve his Utopian dream of a frontier less European nation.

Note: A loose European Union is now a fact with more than 25 member-states including Germany and having a common currency "EURO", while Great Britain retained its Pound-Sterling.

❖❖❖

54. EU'S PLAN FOR KASHMIR

This has reference to the news item "EU Plan on Kashmir Likely". The European Commission in Brussels prepared a policy paper based on which a draft of 'EU Asia Strategy Document' was finalized for discussion by the EU council of heads of states at the 'Aachen Summit' to be held on Dec 9 and 10. It spells out ominous portends for India's Kashmir policy, hanging fire for over four deacdes. The 50-page policy paper of the European Commission deals with strengthening European presence in Asia, by boosting knowledge of European in Asia, opening of markets, improving investment climate, export promotion, strengthening development-cooperation and undertaking a far-and-wide-reaching dialogue on political and security issues both bilaterally and multilaterally. Except the last clause which interferes actively with Indian interests in the Asia-Pacific region, the policy paper, in-so-far as it goes, is good enough. In particular, the Kashmir problem is linked with this notorious last clause of the policy paper.

It seems that the German officials favour a European initiative on Kashmir in the aftermath of rejection of the Pakistani-sponsored draft resolution on Kashmir in the UN General Assembly. The EU seeks to play a positive role in bringing an end to the dispute between India and Pakistan. India has always stood for bilateral talks with Pakistan on the Kashmir question, on the basis of the Simla Accord of 1972. Moves for any intervention by a third party have always been thwarted by India. In this context, EU's initiative to interfere is repugnant to Indian susceptibilities. EU's intervention and internationalization of the Kashmir problem will only complicate matters. If at all, it is a problem in India and Pakistan and could only, be resolved bilaterally and not multilaterally. EU member-states should be firmly informed in no uncertain terms, that India is averse to any possible intervention of a third party on the Kashmir question.

❖❖❖

55. BENAZIR ARMED

This has reference to the editorial 'To Benazir with Love'. The caption is absolutely apt in the sense that the purpose of Ms. Bhutto's US visit, not very long ago, has been eminently fulfilled. President Bill Clinton has gone out of his way to honour his commitments made during her visit, both explicit and implicit.

Republican Senator Larry Pressler's amendment is country-specific. It bars those countries which are engaged in producing nuclear arsenals from receiving American arms and economic aid. Due to this restriction, the US could not provide military and economic aid to Pakistan since 1990. Now the Senate vote for the amendment of Mr. Hank Brown, again a Republican Senator, has struck down the Pressler amendment. It provides President Clinton the much-needed breather.

The US Senate's decision enables Pakistan to receive a massive $ 370 million worth military equipment. This will tilt the military balance in the subcontinent in Pakistan's favour. Though the US turns a Nelson's eye to Pakistan's nuclear ambitions and capabilities, in view of their strategic interests in West Asia and Asia-Pacific region, India cannot and should not do so, as it would be detrimental to its own security needs and its legitimate interests in these regions.

❖❖❖

56. ELECTIONS IN KASHMIR

The Election Commission's decision not to hold elections in Jammu & Kashmir is rather unfortunate. A political decision of the Government has been negated and set aside by a constitutional authority of its own creation. It is a case of the creation challenging the wisdom of its creator. The Government's helplessness before the Election Commission would not wash with the international community, more so, with the US interest and intervention in Kashmir, though extraordinary, thanks to Pakistan's propaganda mill.

Obviously, the Government and the Election Commission viewed the situation from diametrically opposite angles. The Government saw no point in waiting for ideal conditions as such a dispensation would never be possible, given Pakistan's ability to export terrorists trained in its camps, to foment and fuel insurgency in the border State. On the other hand, EC preferred to wait for ideal and peaceful conditions to conduct free and fair elections. But, postponement of elections to a propitious date or cancelling them altogether would not be in national interest.

The Election Commission's decision is bound to have far-reaching consequences. It is certain to please Pakistan which has got sufficient time to carry on its evil designs.

It can be safely argued that the Government's decision of holding polls in Kashmir was itself flawed, if only because the National Conference is opposed to elections at this juncture. It is the only Kashmiri party opposed to secession from India and is secular in its approach. Even though it lost its popularity in the valley, its support base is still intact. Mr. Iftikar Ansari, a senior Congress leader in the valley, who commands great respect from the Shia community which has little or no sympathy with the Sunni-dominated militancy, did emphasis the importance of National Conference in any election in Kashmir.

It is imperative for the Government to take into confidence all the major national Opposition parties and the National Conference and evolve a poll strategy for Kashmir.

❖❖❖

57. INDEPENDENCE OF JUDICIARY

This has reference to the editorial 'Judges, Not Servants'. The press, otherwise known as the Fourth Estate in Westminster parlance, must, by its very nature, be the jealous guardian of the pillars of democracy, of which judiciary is the first and foremost. Viewed in this perspective, your stout defence of judicial independence is commendable and noteworthy. Even so, certain points need to be emphasized in this context.

In theory, the principle of separation of executive and judiciary is a fine ideal. Its implication is that their respective powers should not encroach upon one another. In practice, it is a different story altogether, even in sophisticated western democracies like the USA. In India, judges are appointed by the President on the advice and recommendation of the Union Cabinet of the day. These appointments are not devoid of any influence. In addition, the most significant point is that they are paid from the Consolidated Fund of the Government, just as the other plenipotentiary functionaries of the government. True, the judges are not servants, but, still they are the dignified and exalted employees of the Government. And facts are facts and should be recognised as such.

As against this background, there could be a plethora of valid reasons for the judicial independence to put a check on the executive's otherwise wide and uninhibited powers and balance them to the letter and spirit of the constitution. In this regard, the US constitution is exemplary in its 'checks and balances' over the powers of the executive, parliament and judiciary. We can take a leaf, out of the book of the US constitution and adopt it to our advantage.

Again, there is no such thing as absolute independence. It is always coupled with responsibility and duty.

And the roles of the executive and judiciary are not contradictory but complementary. All said and done, it is to the credit of our judiciary that it kept itself fairly independent from the vagaries of executive interference. It is amply evidenced in its judgment in the matter of a high court judge's pension claim.

❖❖❖

58. EC CROSSING LIMITS

In UK, the parliamentary form of government has graduated into prime ministerial form of government over the years. In this system, it is the privilege and prerogative of the Prime Minister to spring a surprise on the opposition in the matter of holding general elections at a time and date of his choice. And, electoral machinery will duly implement the Prime Minister's decision without let or hindrance.

Free India has adopted Westminster system of democracy lock, stock and barrel. Subject to certain checks and balances of Parliament, the supremacy and pre-eminence of the Prime Minister is unquestionable. Such a construction of Prime Minister's powers has been in evidence, more in actual practice and working, since the days of Mrs. Indira Gandhi. But, of late, it seems the situation has changed.

In this context, the recent moves of the Election Commission are rather disturbing. Its confabulations with all the major national, political parties, including the Congress, with the sole purpose of fixing the date of the general elections is not proper. It is unwittingly trying to abridge and encroach upon the prime ministerial functions. By the same token, it is overstepping its own constitutional functions.

❖❖❖

59. PASSING THE BUCK

Inability coupled with lack of will leads to escapism. This is exactly what has happened over the past few years in the political arena. Judges are suddenly saddled with problems of political import.

Political issues with far-reaching consequences have been conveniently passed on to the judiciary. The Babri Masjid and Ram Janmabhoomi disputes, Cauvery water dispute between Tamil Nadu and Karnataka, the Telecom tenders issue and finally Jain hawala case are a few examples of this in discretion. The judiciary has therefore been compelled to discharge the functions of the executive.

During the days of Mrs. Indira Gandhi, Mr. Rajiv Gandhi and Mr. V.P. Singh, decision-making on political issues was never handed over to the judiciary even inadvertently. The executive and the judiciary functioned within their constitutional limits without trespassing.

With Mr. P.V. Narasimha Rao's advent at the helm of affairs, things have changed radically, with the judiciary achieving more independence. Not only this, but by adjudicating on political matters, the judiciary finds itself an unwilling arbiter in the governance of the country.

There is no doubt that judicial activism has done well to the Indian polity. At the same time, in its functioning.

Democracy, just as ministers, bureaucrats and legislators are subject to criticism and probity, judges should also be subject to public scrutiny. This puts great responsibility on the judiciary. Intellectual exuberance coupled with humility, honesty and impartiality must be the watchwords of the judges and their judicial pronouncements.

❖❖❖

60(a). US REBUFF

The US State Department's rebuff to the Indian embassy, on the supply of ring-magnets (used in uranium enrichment process) to Pakistan by China must serve as a shock-therapy to our policy-makers in South Block. The demarche of the Indian embassy was ill-timed, ill-advised and undiplomatic. The US has asserted that its relations with Pakistan or China are strictly a bilateral matter and it would brook no interference by any third party, least of all India. At least now, India should learn its lesson. To cry hoarse over the US support to Pakistan does not behove an independent nation like India. It is a well-known fact that India does not figure in the US decision-making process over West Asia or Asia-Pacific region. On the other hand, Pakistan is a front-line state and an ally of the US.

The US will overcome its own laws to supply sophisticated military hardware to Pakistan, even if the latter acquires nuclear accessories from China. Brown, amendment to Pressler law, enabling the US to arm Pakistan to its teeth is the latest example. The recent friction in the US-China relations over Taiwan will not change the overall pro-Pakistan policy of the US. India can do nothing about it.

❖❖❖

60(b). MESSAGE FROM THE US

The US State Department's unqualified rebuff to the Indian embassy's overtures on the supply of ring-magnets (used in the uranium enrichment process) to Pakistan by China must serve as a shock-therapy to our policy-makers in South Block.

The demarche of the Indian embassy is ill-timed, ill-advised and undiplomatic.

The US has unequivocally asserted that its relations with Pakistan and with China are strictly bilateral and it would brook no interference by any third party, least of all India. At least now, India should learn its lesson from this unsavoury episode. Always crying itself hoarse over US support to Pakistan does not behove an independent nation like India. Pakistan has always been a front-line state and a friend of the US. That being the case, the US will overcome its own laws to supply sophisticated military hardware to Pakistan, even if Pakistan acquires nuclear accessories from China.

India should learn to act as a free nation in its own interests, in the developing scenario in the sub-continent. It should develop its own nuclear weaponry to meet the threat from across the border and to serve as a deterrent. But it should not try to influence the Indian-Americans in New Jersey or elsewhere to vote in a particular way in the elections to the US Senate or House of Representatives or influence US policies in any manner.

❖❖❖

61. TRUE HINDUTVA

Sir, The BJP's adoption of Hindutva as its election plank reveals its sincerity of purpose. It should be appreciated for its courage of conviction which is, sadly, lacking in almost all political parties without exception. At least the intellectual community and in-depth thinkers will understand the concept for what it stands for, in its proper perspective.

Reflecting on the origin of the words 'Hind' and 'Hindu' would be in order in this context. In ancient times, our subcontinent was referred to, as the land where the river 'Sindh' or 'Sindhu' flowed.

It is a Sanskrit word which means an ocean. Over the years, the word was transformed into 'Hind' or 'Hindu,' by distortion and usage. The sub-continent has thus come to be known as 'Hindudesh' or 'Hindustan' and its people Hindus.

Sindhu was pronounced as Indus by the Greeks, and subsequently by the English. The sub-continent has therefore been referred to as India (The land where the river Indus flows) and its people Indians. It may also be noted that the army of Subhash Chandra Bose was known as 'Azad Hind Fauz' or 'Indian National Army and his slogan was 'Jai Hind'.

It is also true that the word Hindu has come to be ascribed to the followers of the oldest religion in the world, viz., the Vedic religion, the fountainhead of the great epics *Ramayana* and *Mahabharata* and the latter's off-shoot the *Bhagavad Gita*. Some of these followers did change their religion due to historical reasons. Now we find amongst us Muslims, Christians and Buddhists, in the main. All these people are converts from the Hindu or Indian fold. But, all the same, they are all Hindus or Indians. They can call themselves Indian Muslims, Indian Christians and so on.

Reverting to the BJP's Hindutva, there is no reason why anyone should take exception to it, if it means that the people living in India or Hindustan are Indians or Hindus. In fact, the Hindutva concept can cement bonds among all Indian religions and put down fissiparous and separatist tendencies among the people, provided they are educated sufficiently in this aspect.

❖❖❖

62. PRESS AND POLITICAL PARTIES

The BJP, in its election manifesto, has unwittingly promised the electorate to bring out a bill in Parliament to legalize the 'right to reply' of aggrieved persons to unpalatable newspaper reports concerning them. The BJP could have been more circumspect in formulating its manifesto, because this may adversely affect its electoral prospects.

Freedom of the press reflects freedom of expression and the press is the conscience-keeper of any nation. If any political party tries to interfere with it by any means, it will boomerang on it.

Throttling of the press by the former PM, Indira Gandhi, during the emergency period and the consequent virtual rout of the Congress in the 1977 parliamentary elections is a glaring and outstanding example of such a scenario.

In the UK, they follow established conventions in this regard. Here in India, there are no conventions to guide the interaction of the press and the political parties. It is, therefore, advisable for them to come to a compromise defining their respective roles unambiguously. If necessary, they may sign a memorandum of understanding (MoU) to this effect, as the frequency of trespassing on each other's domain of activities is on the increase.

❖❖❖

63. CONGRESS-BSP ALLIANCE

It is said that politics is the art of the possible and there are no fast friends or fast enemies in politics. This dictum is amply in evidence in the Congress-BSP alliance in UP for the forthcoming assembly elections there. Detractors of the Congress may call it a marriage of convenience or even opportunism, while its supporters may call it a masterstroke.

In this context, one still remembers with disgust and remorse, the damage done to Mahatma Gandhi's samadhi in Rajghat by the followers of Mr. Kanshi Ram, the BSP supremo. One wonders if Gandhiji, the apostle of peace and non-violence, who gave the country its freedom and its flag and acclaimed as "the kingliest of kings" by Sarojini Naidu (the Nightingale of India), could be subjected to this kind of vandalism. But, the Congress government headed by Mr. P.V. Narasimha Rao turned a Nelson's eye to this incident, even though there were a few muffled protests of sorts by some Congressmen. The P.V. government must have thought that discretion is the better part of valour. Even now, this incident did not come in the way of Congress joining hands with BSP. The Congress seems to have seen virtue in vice, in striking the deal with BSP. Politics is played for power at all costs, throwing ideologies to the winds. One only hopes that this alliance in UP would not meet the fate of Congress—AIADMK alliance in Tamil Nadu.

❖❖❖

64. AFGHAN CRISIS

Afghanistan has been bleeding since Red Army overran it in 1979 to bring it under Soviet sphere of influence. Subsequently, the hapless country became a pawn in the superpower chessboard of rivalry.

Mr. Gulbuddin Hekmatyar was armed to the teeth by the US, through the conduit of Pakistan to fight the Afghan Government. After 18 years of armed struggle, Mr. Hekmatyar realised the futility of militancy in the face of more powerful Taliban militia, which was bent on overthrowing President Burhanuddin Rabbani.

He made truce with his arch-rival, Mr. Rabbani, to become the Afghan Prime Minister, a thorny job.

Afghanistan's woes are mainly due to Pakistan's interference in that country's affairs by supporting insurgency. If only Pakistan stops its unsolicited fishing in Afghanistan's troubled waters, then peace would be possible in that country.

❖❖❖

65. WHEN JUDICIAL ACTIVISM IS GOOD?

The words 'judicial activism', very much in vogue now, refer to the judiciary's over-sensitive attitude and activity in all and sundry matters, not necessarily in their jurisdiction. PIL or public interest litigation has come in handy for the judiciary to enter the domain of activities which are not their preserve. It must, however, be said in all fairness to the judiciary that this scenario is not of its own making.

The prevarication and procrastination, and consequent inaction of the executive over the country's myriad problems is mainly responsible for this ambiguous situation. Successive Prime Ministers have found it convenient to throw knotty problems of politics at the doors of judiciary, because they do not have the political will to find amicable solutions to these problems. The judiciary, in turn, found it saddled with problems foreign to the realm of its jurisdiction, but thought it prudent to pronounce judgments on matters of State. This is certainly an unhealthy trend.

The roles of the executive, legislature and judiciary have been clearly defined and demarcated in our Constitution. Trespass by any one of them into another's region of activity is not conducive to democratic functioning; in fact, it strikes at the very roots of democracy, vesting more powers in one of its organs, to the deprivation of the other two.

The prevailing situation thrusts supreme responsibility on the judicial system. Judges should be extremely careful and circumspect in decision-making. For this purpose, they should be men of character who can avoid temptations. In fact, they should emulate Plato's 'Philosopher King'. As the famous Telugu poet Yogi Vemana said, even the creator Brahma could be tempted and lured by money and women. It is well if judges avoid these pitfalls. In that ideal situation, judicial activism will be good for the country.

❖❖❖

66. JUDICIAL ACCOUNTABILITY

Much has been said and written on the phenomenon of 'judicial activism'. Even so, much desired has been left out. In fact, no serious attempt has ever been made to dwell on the human tragedies that are the direct consequences of law's delays, indecision and perversion.

The most pathetic instance in this context is that of biscuit king Rajen Pillai of Singapore. He was brought into this country to be tried for his economic offences, if any. The designated trial court in Delhi, assuming the airs of medical profession, ruled that he needed no medical check-up. The very next day he expired, obviously due to lack of medical attention.

Another notable case is that of Sanjay Dutt, hero of Bollywood. He was arrested under TADA, due to his supposed involvement in the violent disturbances in Bombay in the aftermath of the demolition of the Babri Masjid in Ayodhya. The designated TADA court in Bombay was unable to take a decision on his bail petition. In consequence, the petition was passed on from one court to another including the Supreme Court. After a lapse of over a year or so, it was finally decided that he could be granted bail. Due to this prevarication and procrastination, the particular individual not only suffered untold mental agony but also lost ground in his lucrative career in the cine field. No responsibility has ever been fixed for these lapses on the part of the judiciary. People talk of accountability for the commissions and omissions of the executive wing, law enforcement agency, political wing and bureaucracy. As judiciary is also one of the wings of democracy, it cannot be immune to the concept of accountability. When once the spectre of accountability looms large over their coveted ethics and conduct, their decision-making could be fool-proof and might not result in pathetic human tragedies.

❖❖❖

67(a). GUJRAL DOCTRINE IS HARMFUL

Ever since I.K. Gujral took over as Prime Minister, opposition leaders are expressing concern over the so-called Gujral doctrine. It envisages unilateral offer of concessions to the neighbouring countries with a view to establish and improve good relations with them. Ms. Rabin Raphel, former US Assistant Secretary of state, commended it.

Though Gujral's name has come to be attached to this liberal approach in foreign affairs, it is being actually practised by leaders for quite a long time with adverse results, even before independence of this country.

In the pre-independence days, the Congress under the leadership of Gandhi, Nehru and Patel used to appease and prop up Jinnah with unilateral concessions. The result was partition of the country. In the post-independence days, Nehru gave up again unilaterally India's rights and interests in Tibet to appease China, without obtaining matching concessions on McMohan Line, the Indo-Tibetan border and the result was that Chinese PLA overran Tibet. Not only this. The Chinese army overran McMohan Line in Oct 1962, claiming large tracts of Indian Territory in the North-eastern region.

Again in the December 1971 Indo-Pak war, though India won decisively, Indira Gandhi gave up the fruits of success by unilaterally conceding and returning all the areas taken over by Indian Army on the Western front and also returned over 90,000 POWs to Pakistan. In a war, the victor takes all and leaves nothing to the vanquished. This dictum was overlooked by Mrs. Gandhi for the sake of good neighbourly relations with Pakistan. And the result was the low-intensity war thrust by Pakistan in the Kashmir valley in the late eighties. All this is past history of unilateral concessions.

National interests must reign supreme in the conduct of foreign relations. Viewed in this perspective, according unilateral concessions to neighbours to befriend them is not in India's interest.

And so the "Gujral doctrine" should be committed to the dust bin and India's interests saved, protected and defended.

❖❖❖

67(b). FRIEND TO FOE POLICY

Ever since Mr. I.K. Gujral took over as the PM, opposition leaders have voiced their concern on the so-called Gujral doctrine. It envisages unilateral offer of concessions to the neighbouring countries with a view to establish and improve good relations with them. Though Gujral's name has been attached with this approach to foreign affairs, it was being practiced by our leaders for quite a long time with adverse results, even before independence.

The Congress under the Gandhi, Nehru and Patel used to appease Jinnah with unilateral concessions. The result was partition and the birth of theocratic Pakistan. Post-independence, Nehru gave up India's rights and interests in Tibet to China, without obtaining matching concessions on the McMohan Line, the Indo-Tibetan border and the result was that Chinese PLA overran Tibet and the Line as well in 1962, claiming large tracts of Indian Territory. In Dec 1971's Indo-Pak war, though India won decisively, Indira Gandhi surrendered the fruits of success, by conceding and returning areas taken by the Indian Army on the Western front. Indira Gandhi overlooked the victory for neighbourly relations with Pakistan. The result, a low-intensity war by Pakistan in the Kashmir valley in the late eighties. If national interests must reign supreme, then unilateral concessions to neighbours is not in India's interests. The so-called Gujral doctrine so should be ignored and India's interests saved.

❖❖❖

68. DEMOLITIONS FOR WB AID

This is to highlight the havoc and horror created by the State government in Godavari districts. In the name of removal of encroachments and widening the highways, complete buildings were destroyed. Quite a few people lost their lives unable to withstand the tragedy and trauma of these horrendous deeds while the press and political parties looked the other way.

Amalapuram and Peddapuram in East Godavari and Bhimavaram, Penugonda, Palacole and Nidadavole in West Godavari were scenes of vast destruction and devastation. All this is done by the government ostensibly to obtain World Bank loan. People are seething with anger but are helpless in the face of the government's dictatorial methods. It seems as if the government is carrying a well organized war on its own people. The NHRC should take note of this fact and initiate measures to alleviate the common man's suffering.

❖❖❖

69. WHENCE DEMOCRACY?

The turn of events in Pakistan is a pointer to the unfolding scenario of a possible military intervention, in the near future. In the tug-of-war between Chief Justice Sajjad Ali Shah, Prime Minister Nawaz Sharif and President Farooq Leghari, it is Nawaz Sharif who has come out unscathed. Army chief Gen. Jahangir Karamat has thrown his weight behind Sharif, making the position of the other two dignitaries untenable. Thus, the army has become the final arbiter in Pakistan's guided democracy. And, the army has firmly entrenched itself once again in Pakistan's politics.

Pakistan's ex-Chief Justice had dared to challenge the Prime Minister by instituting contempt-of-court proceeding against him for his alleged remarks against the Chief Justice. Nawaz Sharif met the army chief and discussed the issue.

Nobody knows what transpired in these confabulations so far. By implication, this means that both the CJ and the PM have invited the army to settle the dispute between them. With the resignation of President Leghari, politics in Pakistan have come back to square one.

The army is ruling the country with a facade of civilian presence under a Cabinet system. This was going on since the untimely demise of Gen Zia-ul-Haq in 1987 in an air crash.

Indeed, some credit should go to Sajjad Ali Shah, who unwittingly became the first Chief Justice of Pakistan, to give the Prime Minister a real scare. His daring attitude is comparable to that of Justice Jag Mohanlal Sinha of Allahabad High Court, who set aside the election of Indira Gandhi, the then PM, to parliament, from Rae Bareilly. All said and done, democracy can exist only when its three wings, the executive, judiciary and legislature function in harmony. This applies to Pakistan as well.

❖❖❖

70. WRONGLY CRUCIFIED

Subsequent to the withdrawal of support to the United Front government by the Congress, certain sections of the press branded the Congress as anti-national.

Such allegations are absolutely unjustified. It is a sad comment on any political party, leave alone the Congress, which has a proud record of nationalism for over 112 years, since its birth on December 28, 1885. Before apportioning a label to any political party, one should define nationalism and nation-state, in the Indian context.

To support or not support a rainbow coalition that the UF is, lies certainly within the domain of decision-making in the Congress party. And the Congress does not become anti-national overnight by its decision. It is because politics is the game played for power. If Congress uses Sonia to gain ascendancy and power, it is not committing any crime. Many are raising a hue and cry over the fact that Sonia is an Italian. It is to be remembered that the Indian society is itself devastatingly cosmopolitan, with foreign elements being Indianised progressively since time immemorial. To exemplify this scenario, one should know that Chandragupta Maurya married the daughter of Greek warrior Selucus. No one ever called him anti-national. In fact, he goes down in history as one of the greatest emperors. Many races like the Huns from Germany and the religious followers of Buddhism, Mohammadamism, Jainism and Persians were merged in the Indian society and Indianised.

❖❖❖

71(a). NOW, POLL PANEL ACTIVISM

The Election Commission is one of the four wings of democracy, the other three being the executive, legislature and judiciary. Of these, the judiciary has already crossed its functional domain, as ordained by the Constitution. This phenomenon has come to be known as "judicial activism" in the press parlance. Now, since the time of T.N. Seshan, the Election Commission has also crossed the limits of its well-defined functions. This aberration can also be called Election Commission activism.

The main function of the Election Commission is to conduct parliamentary and assembly elections, whenever they are due. It can also recognize or derecognize political parties based on their performance in the general elections. It did perform these duties admirably, so far since the first general elections in 1952. Of late, it is questioning the political parties' constitutional provisions and functions. It has entered the domain of their organizational elections, which is purely their internal matter. It is questioning their principles and functions, their Magna Carta for the people, in essence. This is unabashed interference in the internal matters of the political parties. The EC notices to the TDP and Shiv Sena are the latest examples.

Any political party has the fundamental right to formulate its own policies and programmes in respect of home (internal) and foreign affairs. The EC has no business to question the fundamentals of any party. It is certainly outside the EC jurisdiction. It is hoped that the EC would avoid crossing its constitutional limits and obligations.

❖❖❖

71(b). EC ACTIVISM

The Election Commission is one of the four wings of democracy, the other three being the executive, legislature and judiciary. Of these, the judiciary has already crossed its functional domain, as ordained by the Constitution; this phenomenon has come to be known as 'judicial activism'. Now, since the departure of Seshan, the EC has also crossed the limits of its well-defined functions. As in the case of judiciary, this aberration can also be called EC activism. The main function of the Commission is to conduct Parliamentary and Assembly elections, whenever they are due. It can also recognize or derecognize political parties based on their performance in the general elections. Well, it did perform these duties admirably well, so far, since the first general elections in 1952. Of late, it is questioning the political parties' constitutional provisions and functions.

It has entered the domain of their organisational elections. It is, in essence, questioning their principles and their Magna Carta. This is unabashed interference in the internal matters of the political parties. Recent targets of such interference are the TDP and Shiv Sena. Any political party has the fundamental right to formulate its own programmes in respect of homeland and foreign policies. The EC has no business questioning the fundamentals on any party.

❖❖❖

72. TORMENTOR-IN-CHIEF OF VAJPAYEE GOVERNMENT

To run a coalition government is difficult. More so, if the partners are intransigent. In general, it is formed and run with a common minimum programme acceptable to all its constituent partners. Obviously, the BJP-led coalition government has no such programme in the first place. Secondly, coalition partners seek a pound of flesh now and then from the BJP, for extending their support to the government. Of course, the BJP's main tormentor has been AIADMK supremo Jayalalitha. It is as if she runs the government by remote control from Chennai. That, in spite of all these troubles, the government could stay in power for more than one year is a miracle of sorts.

The present predicament of the Vajpayee government resembles an episode in the epic *Mahabharat*. As per the promise given to Yudhishtir, Salya, the 'saradhi/charioteer' of Karna, runs down the latter with derogatory remarks on his prowess in archery and torments him in the two-day battle fought by Karna against Arjun whose 'saradhi' was Lord Krishna Himself. It is said that Salya's remarks were one of the main reasons for the defeat and death of Karna, in the hands of Arjun. Based on this episode, a proverb 'Salya

Saradhyam' came into vogue in many languages, particularly in Telugu. Anybody who acts (in word and deed) against the interests of his friend is said to be doing 'Salya Saradhyam'. Drawing an anology, if Vajpayee is Karna then Jayalalitha would be the female-counterpart of Salya. And the present political episode is complete.

Right now, it seems the Vajpayee government's days are numbered. Eventually, it may fall or may not fall. But already, many a Barkis (a fictional character) like Deve Gowda is too willing to don the mantle of the next prime minister, in case another coalition government is formed in place of the existing one. But, no other coalition government is possible, given the present composition of the Lok Sabha. Thus, yet another general election may be thrust on the people, a third since 1996. And main responsibility for the same would have to be borne by the AIADMK supremo.

❖❖❖

73. INEPT HANDLING

This has reference to the editorial, 'Dancing with the Wolves' on the hijacking episode. The government has danced to the tune of the terrorists. It has proved itself inept in crisis management which requires control of the situation and quick decision-making. It miserably failed on these two accounts. By its inexplicable indecision, it lost control of the situation in Amritsar airport, thus forsaking the major advantage of exercising the military option.

Events overtook the government in quick succession jeopardizing all its maneuverability. And eventually, it succumbed to the manipulations of the Taliban-assisted hijackers. In the process, it had to release three top terrorists to obtain the release of the hapless passengers of IC-814 aircraft from the clutches of the hijackers. No doubt, it was the best of a bad bargain. Obviously, wisdom, if any, had dawned on the government after the bungling at Amritsar and after it was too late.

Now, the question is, why should the terrorists, captured by our security forces at considerable risk to their lives, should be handed over to the hijackers? It seems that our soldiers lost their precious lives during the Kargil war with Pakistan for nothing. The government's first and foremost duty is to protect and save the lives of all its citizens. It has singularly failed in this primary duty. It has not remembered the blood of India's martyred sons at the altar of various wars with Pakistan while striking a deal with the blackmailers.

The aftermath of the hijack will be far-reaching in its ramifications. India's vulnerability in the face of organized terrorism is now an open secret. Terrorists will be encouraged to intensify their nefarious activities in Kashmir. The armed forces may be demoralized. Their leadership will have a difficult job of convincing the rank and file, of their continued need to sacrifice lives in fighting and apprehending the terrorists. The government has to take the responsibility of boosting the morale of the armed forces. And the struggle against terrorism has to be continued with renewed vigour to keep India united. Eternal vigil on the borders is a pre-requisite to eliminate terrorism.

74. ASYLUM FOR KARMAPA

The defection of the teenaged Karmapa Ugyen Trinley Dorjee into India on January 5 from his monastery in Lasha has come close on the heels of the hijack episode by Pakistani nationals. Though, there is no correlation between the two events, Vajpayee government's indecision so far, in granting political asylum to Karmapa Lama will be viewed with critical interest, in view of its inept handling of the hijack affair.

The real reason for Karmapa's flight to safety and shelter through Himalayan ranges, remains an enigma wrapped in mystery. It may be due to the continuing suppression of the culture and heritage coupled with the abuse of human rights of Tibetans.

Without losing much time, China delivered a veiled warning to India exhorting it not to play host to the boy-monk. By doing so, China has conveyed by implication that it has played no part in the escape-episode of Karmapa. It is case of double-cross to make us leave in a make-believe heaven.

It seems that Karmapa has conveyed to the Indian government through Dalai Lama, his desire to stay on in India and seek political asylum. In this context, it must be remembered that India and Tibet have close historical and cultural relations since time immemorial. In our Puranas, Tibet is quoted as Tripishtapam, the abode of 'Devatas'. At present, about 1,30,000 Tibetan refugees live in India. Karmapa Lama leads the Kagyu School of Buddhism which has a large following spread all over the world. The Kagyu sect has its headquarters at the Rumtek monastery in Sikkim, which houses the Black Hat, the symbol of authority of the sect.

There are media reports that the government may not agree to provide asylum to Karmapa so as not to offend China, as we have already on hand a difficult problem of combating Pakistan-sponsored terrorism in Kashmir and elsewhere. True, we cannot afford to fight on two fronts–one with Pakistan in the west and the other with China in the north. But, already a military alliance exists between China and Pakistan and is directed against India. China is claiming large tracts of our territory in Arunachal Pradesh. It has not recognized the merger of Sikkim with India. Its antagonism towards India is decades old. India should not act under a fear-psychosis. It is India's moral responsibility to grant asylum to Karmapa Lama, in keeping with its best traditions of hospitality.

Note: Subsequently, China has okayed Sikkim's merger with India, at a later date.

❖❖❖

75. THEY NEED FOOD, CLOTHING, NOT IT

The recently concluded 'Janmabhoomi Programme' was conducted with much fanfare. The ministerial extravaganza had necessitated huge public expenditure that could have been easily avoided. Instead of each of the ministers doling out temporary benefits like mechanical appliances, pension and the like to the needy public, the work could have been entrusted to the district collectors. The ministers should, as a rule, confine themselves to their offices in the capital to get involved in the decision-making process and get the decisions implemented by their staff. But this was not to be. They are certainly engaged in their image-building exercise in the name of various programmes.

In addition, a sort of census operation, called micro-survey, was undertaken, by making the teachers and students participate in this exercise. In the process, students have lost their study hours and teachers their teaching hours.

It is well known that these programmes are envisaged and planned under 'Vision 2020 Document', prepared by an Australian consultant, Mr. Mackenzie. This document advocates development of existing resources and promotion of capital-intensive agricultural methods, namely agro-based industries and inputs for them. Development of agriculture was not its aim. It is for promotion of private sector in all fields. Already in tune, education, electricity, health-care and social service sectors are undergoing privatization.

The document does not take into account the ground realities in Andhra Pradesh. There are, at present, about two crore people below the poverty line. There are lakhs of educated unemployed and their number would increase by leaps and bounds in the coming months and years. It does not indicate how employment opportunities could be created and multiplied in the next 20 years.

The government speaks of taking information technology to the grassroots. Large sections of people are illiterate, poverty-stricken and downtrodden. To say that information technology would be useful to them is absurd. First, the government should take measures to feed them, clothe them and house them and then only, it can talk of information technology, electronic governance and all that goes with them.

A work-force of educated-unemployed could be formed and utilized with proper training in all the government programmes like census operations, preparation of voters' lists and family planning drive.

Uninterrupted power supply is a must for the development of industries either agricultural or otherwise. Without achieving self-sufficiency in the power sector, no progress can be made in any sector and Swarna Andhra Pradesh will be an illusion and not a reality, even after 50 years hence.

❖❖❖

76. SHOULD LAWYERS TAKE TO STREETS?

The editorial, 'Expulsion of Dissent' takes a dim view on lawyers' agitation against the amendments proposed by the government to C.P.C. and Advocates' Act. It has been rightly said that they should fight their battles in the courtroom. This, by implication, means that they should not rush into the streets for redressal of their grievances, if any, keeping in view of the high traditions of their profession. By resorting to agitational methods, they make themselves look 'small' in the eyes of the public and lower their image. Instead of agitating, they could have easily argued and discussed the issues with the government to decide upon mutually agreed solutions.

Nevertheless, the amendment incorporating "periodic assessment of lawyer's ability" in Advocates Act is unwarranted. This is being and will be done more efficiently and ruthlessly by their clients. No litigant ever goes to an incompetent lawyer for the redressal of his grievances through the courts. The government need not worry on this account.

Regarding inordinate delays in litigation, even the greatest of English playwrights 'William Shakespeare' spoke of "Law's delays and insolence of office" in the soliloquy of 'Hamlet, the Prince of Denmark'. Though justice delayed is justice denied, reducing the number of appeals would not be conducive to and would not contribute to unadulterated and truthful justice; this is more so, because no amount of infallibility can be attributed with any certainty, to any single judge. The government should have a rethink on this matter.

To reduce the load on the high courts, a number of high court benches could be created in each state. In the same manner, subordinate judge's courts may be set up in all prominent towns. This will contribute to absorption of more suitable advocates as judges. When there are a number of universities and colleges in each nook and corner of each state, there is a strong case for establishing more courts as well for the benefit of the litigant public. This will also considerably reduce the laws' delays.

On the question of the entry of foreign lawyers into Indian courts, it will increase the competitivity among lawyers, foreign or indigenous. It will, in turn, lead lo achieving excellence and perfection, in the pursuit of their profession. This will immensely benefit both the lawyers and the litigants. And, on this score, the government should go ahead with the concerned legislation.

77. THE BLACK TUESDAY

Last Tuesday, I watched on TV in disbelief, the collapse of the twin towers of the World Trade centre and part of Pentagon. That the terrorists could attack the citadels of the US economic power and military might by using civilian planes with ease and impunity is a matter of serious concern to all the democratic nations. It is surprising that the most vigilant and powerful intelligence agencies like FBI and CIA of the US could not anticipate and nip in the bud the terrorist plan of attack.

America's conventional weaponry and nuclear arms proved to be no deterrence to the well-planned attacks of the terrorists with minimum expenditure. In this perspective, the US will have to rethink and revise its project of National Missile Defense (NMD), because it cannot be a bulwark of defence against terrorist attacks of murder and mayhem. No doubt, the US would retaliate with its full military might against the perpetrators of terror against its citizens. It had already pointed out its needle of suspicion against Osama bin Laden, the fugitive Arab jihadi living in Afghanistan. Preparations are in full swing to resort to air strikes on his terrorist training camps in Afghanistan. In this scenario, even though India itself was bitten and bled, for over a decade by cross-border terrorism sponsored by Pakistan, it could play no effective role unless asked for by the US. So far, no such demarche had come from the US. India had no other option but to wait and see the developing situation as it emerges.

❖❖❖

78. PEOPLES' WILL

The editorial 'Good Riddance' on Jayalalithaa's discomfiture is forthright and well-reasoned. Even so, some points need to be elaborated, emphasized and highlighted.

The observation of the Supreme Court that the peoples' will is subservient to the Constitution is debatable. The Constitution itself reflects and is based on the will of the people. It is constructed and made by the peoples' representatives, for the people. As such, it is beyond anybody's comprehension as to how people's will could be subjected and subordinated to checks and balances of the Constitution, because people's will is supreme.

Your guess and suggestion that the Constitution was silent on the need to keep convicts out of power because such a provision would have acted against men like Nehru and Patel occupying positions of power as they were convicted many times under Cr PC, is certainly farfetched and outlandish. The founding fathers of the Constitution could not anticipate and envisage that a time would come when persons of dubious character and with criminal records would aspire and occupy public positions by exploiting the so-called ambiguities in its letter and spirit. As per Nehru and Patel, they were freedom fighters. If they were convicted, it was because they were fighting for the freedom of the country from foreign yoke and not on corruption or criminal charges. Any comparison of these stalwarts, with the present-day pygmy politicians, even remotely, would be outrageous. You have, however, admitted this much when you said it would be sacrilegious.

❖❖❖

79. DEMOCRACY IN BANGLA

The Bangladesh Begums Sheikh Hasina Wajed and Khalida Zia fought a pitched battle with no holds barred in the recently concluded general elections. There is no reason to believe that the elections were rigged. In fact, they were conducted in an orderly and peaceful manner but for a few incidents of violence. Bangladesh's image as one of the very few democracies in the Islamic world has been established.

Scant attention was paid in India towards the elections in Bangladesh. India was always preoccupied in countering and checkmating Pakistan's manoeuvers, diplomatic or otherwise; all the policies of India are basically Pakistan-centred, conditioned as they are. Even so, India has to take cognizance of the change of guard in Bangla, irrespective of the person who guides the destiny of that nation. Dhaka's cooperation is very essential and vital for India to counter the internal insurgency threats in its North-eastern states. Also, India has to conduct negotiations with Dhaka to delineate the common boundary. There is again the problem of adverse possession of territorial enclaves on either side of crying for solution. In addition, India is virtually the only neighbour of Bangladesh. And, in view of the outstanding problems quoted above, both India and Bangladesh have to conduct their mutual relations amicably and in a conducive manner, irrespective of any change of Government in either country. In this context, the onus and responsibility rests more or less on India, in the sense that it should overcome its lethargy and engage the countries to the east of its geographical location, including Bangladesh to achieve fruitful cooperation and useful friendship with them.

❖❖❖

80. SUICIDE CAR BOMB

In the aftermath of the suicide car bomb attack on J&K Assembly, Chief Minister Farooq Abdullah lamented about the inaction of India in the face grave threats. He questioned whether India would act only after Kashmir, has perished. India was saddled with cross-border terrorist attacks for more than a decade. But no concrete steps were initiated except, issuing condolence statements and then requesting the US administration to restrain Pakistan to cease smuggling trained into terrorists into Kashmir. The US considered Pakistan a front-line state and a bulwark against the Soviet Union during the Cold War period. Now, when it was subjected to malicious terrorist attacks, Pakistan was again restored to the earlier status. It was India's experience that during the three wars thrust upon it by Pakistan the US military hardware was used against it.

The US strikes on Afghanistan maybe successful in their limited aim but, it is no comfort to India. The US is not interested in admonishing Pakistan for its role in Kashmir imbroglio. Nobody will come to India's aid in its fight against terrorism in Kashmir and elsewhere. India should learn to fight its battles on its own. If possible, the terrorist breeding camps in PoK across the line of control should be destroyed by whatever means available. India should convert, the opportunity that has emerged at present to its advantage and act with equanimity and firmness to eradicate the decade-long disease of terrorism in Kashmir. An opportunity, comes very rarely and once in a lifetime. If we fail to utilise it to our benefit, we are lost in mid-stream and cannot be retrieved again.

❖❖❖

81. THE GAINER

The Anglo-American war on terror against Afghanistan began with 'all sound and fury'. But as days advanced, it seems that the US has developed cold feet and its terror-war lost its full steam. This phenomenon is perhaps, due to the incontrovertible fact that each of the grand coalition partners cobbled up by the UK and the US have their own axe to grind. In consequence, fissures have developed between them on the question of post-Taliban scenario in Afghanistan.

Russia is of the view that fighting terrorism by striking at its fruit with a stick, instead of reaching for its roots, will be foolhardy. It regards Taliban as a threat to Central Asia. And, it feels that Taliban and Al Queda should be fought on the ground in association and in tandem with the Afghan opposition Northern Alliance forces. Towards this end, Russia has stepped up armament supplies to these forces. But, the US is wary of doing so, as the Northern Alliance would have a disproportionate leverage in the formation of a new government when Taliban meets its doom. This was corroborated by the British Foreign Secretary Jackistraw when he declared that Mullah Omar and his faction cannot, simply, be replaced by another narrow faction. Obviously, Russia and the US are working at cross-purposes.

The US perspective is that moderate Taliban elements could be accommodated in any future broad-based multi-ethnic Government in Afghanistan, if only to satisfy and salvage the concerns of Pakistan, the creator of Taliban. But Russia along with India and Iran would not countenance such a proposition, as there would be no moderates in the obscurantist setup of Taliban. The course of military operations would be affected by these rumblings and rivalry between the US and Russia. And, it is the Taliban who could gain some military advantage and hence some political space in the bargain.

❖❖❖

82. PARLIAMENT ATTACK

With reference to the edit on the attack on Parliament, it was written with, platonic favour, reflecting the sentiments of all Indians. By all accounts, it is gratifying to note that our security personnel acted with commendable alertness, bravery and firmness risking their own lives and in the process, averting a major catastrophe. The cataclysmic potential of such attacks is astonishing in their accuracy, brevity and precision. A case in point is the dare-devil terrorist attack on the Kashmir Assembly on October 01. And, we are caught unawares by the militant blitzkrieg. The reason is that we wake up only after the event without caring to draw appropriate lessons when the earlier event occurred and implementing necessary security-checks to obviate the probability of yet another such event taking place. Our pathological inaction all these years led to the loss of precious lives of innocent civilians and military personnel on duty. At least now, it is time, for pro-active action against the terrorist menace. Success often comes to those who dare and act. Let us not procrastinate the day of reckoning in striking at the roots of militancy, instead of beating about the 'Bush'.

❖❖❖

83. COOL MINDS *VS.* HOT HEADS

With reference to the Editorial 'Cool Minds *vs.* Hot Hauls', the edit has hypothesized that ultimately non-military options will prove more effective than military option. Permit me to say that this is not based on an in-depth appreciation of the history of war and peace. It is said that peace is an interval, sometime prolonged, between two wars. Be it as it may, we have not exhausted all our military options. We are so far engaged often times, only in defensive operations, countering the enemy attacks and repulsing them, of course very successfully. We have not employed any other option till now. That being the case, we have to explore the possibility of using the offensive option against the enemy, since offensive is the best defense in military parlance. India's earlier experience when it approached the UN on the issue of Pakistan's aggression on Kashmir in 1947 was not very flattering. The aggressor and the aggrieved were put on equal footing and Kashmir was rendered a contentious issue between the two. It would not, therefore, be any different now. We have to go about and implement our own unfinished agenda to decimate the terrorist menace, without worrying about the reactions of others including the Americans.

In the finishing touches of the editorial, it is rightly postulated that finally it is the cool mind that wins and not the hot head absolutely true. The cool thinking is required even to win a war, rather than physical prowess and arms build-up. Napoleon rightly said that, even in war, moral is to the physical as 10 to 1.

❖❖❖

84. NO LOOSE WORDS

With reference to the editorial 'Loose Words' on the Chief of Army Staff (COAS) Gen. S. Padmanabhan's press conference, it is unduly critical and uncharitable. The General has only informed the press about the preparedness of the Armed Forces for all eventualities. This was absolutely necessary to boost the morale of the soldiers and people. The General must have given due deliberation and thought to the various parameters involved, before interaction with the press. And so, the words used were weighty and not loose in any sense and by any stretch of imagination.

The General's combative mood reflected in his remarks was indeed necessary to counter the sabre rattling of President Musharraf and his Press Secretary Rashid Qureshi, day-in and day-out. Even our government leaders were engaged in a war of words with the leaders of Pakistan, ever since the ghastly incident of Dec 13.

Much ado was cognizable in the edit on the General's views on India's Nuclear capability. He reaffirmed India's commitment to 'No-first-use' of nuclear weaponry. He, however, made the point that India would launch 'a second-strike'. As Pakistan's leaders never ruled out the first-strike, the General was within his right to express his views on a possible nuclear warfare.

❖❖❖

85. WITHDRAWAL SYMPTOMS

The editorial 'Withdrawal Symptoms' suffers from an excessive reliance on Pakistan's four-fold proposals for de-escalation of tensions. These are intended for the US consumption. President Bush has already patted Musharraf, on the back. Pakistan's troops were moved to the forward positions along the border and LoC in particular, to facilitate the infiltration of their terrorist freedom fighters into the Kashmir Valley. If it were not the case, they would have been withdrawn to their normal positions, once the ritual of periodic exercise was over. As this was not done, the Indian troops were also moved to the forward positions to meet and withstand any misadventure by Pakistan's Army. In this context, the edit question "Can't the Pakistani troops stop movement of terrorists" smacks of naivety.

Our troops are deployed on the border, firstly to check the infiltration of terrorists from Pakistan and secondly, to apply military pressure on Pakistan so that it may take corrective steps to contain and eliminate the export of trained terrorists across the border. Unless these two missions are fulfilled, it would be foolhardy to withdraw our troops from the border as desired by Pakistan. As regards the restoration of air, rail and road links, it would be wise on our part, to accede to this suggestion. In respect of the UN military observers group on the border, there should be no beefing it up and it should be advised to wind up its activities. Furthermore, we should ask the human rights' groups and international media to highlight the abuse of human rights in Pakistan and in PoK, in particular. Pakistan need not worry about India's human rights record.

❖❖❖

86. HELP AFGHANISTAN

Kuldip Nayar's article 'Kabul Calling' reflects Indian urge for friendly and viable relations with Afghanistan. It refers to the Indian connection to Afghanistan dating back to the Rig-Veda period. It was stated that the Rig-Veda hymns mention two rivers Kubha (Kabul) and Suvastu (Swat) amongst other references like 'Avesta' (Afghanistan). It was also mentioned that the Magadh emperor

Ashoka spread Budhism in Afghanistan. In this context, I would like to add another parameter, viz., in the great epic *Mahabharata*, there was mention of King Subala of Gandhara (the present-day Kandahar) whose daughter Gandhari was given in marriage to the Kuru emperor Dhrutarashtra. So, the connection goes even beyond the Vedic period, to the epic times. However, these prehistoric connections would be of no great avail and use to India, if it could not utilize the present opportunity to its advantage by helping Afghanistan to build up from the scratch, left-over by the Taliban destruction.

Again, a point was made that Afghanistan has been part and parcel of South Asian ethos both by virtue of history and culture, referring to the resolution adopted by some 500 men and women of South Asia. Even, the epics point out, to this fact. And so, it is for consideration in the fitness of the matter that Afghanistan may be included as a seventh member-state in SAARC organization for deriving mutual benefit.

❖❖❖

87. CONTEMPT OF COURT

The editorial 'Gratuitous Attack on Judges' maintains a studied and stoic balance on the Booker Prize winner and NBA activist Arundhati Roy's symbolic incarceration for her alleged criminal contempt of court. The Supreme Court had, once again proved, if proof was necessary, that even the high and the mighty would not escape its admonition and censure.

There is something amiss in the whole episode. The law of criminal contempt is an extraordinary legal provision vested with the Courts, to deal with extraordinary situations and to be used only sparingly. It is neither intended to suppress criticism of court judgments nor discourage free and frank expression of speech and writing. It is very rarely used by the courts in the UK. In the US also, it is invoked only in the rarest of the rare cases. But in India, it seems that our courts are bent upon taking recourse to it more often than not to uphold their dignity. Indiscriminate use of contempt law jurisdiction may impinge and lower the dignity of courts; this in turn, may lead the public to losing confidence in the courts' justice. The courts should, therefore, welcome rather than resent fair and objective criticism of their judgments with equanimity and grace. The dignity of courts should rest on firm foundations instead of contempt laws.

❖❖❖

88. ARMED FORCES

The goings-on in the Armed Forces leave much to be desired. Politicking in the higher echelons of this institution seems to have crept in slowly but surely. A case in point is that of Air Marshall Manjit Singh Sekhon, one of the senior-most officers heading the Southern Air Command. He had to resign, on the ground that he sought political prop for his career advancement, which was incompatible with his official status. Sukhdev Singh Dhindsa, Union Minister (Akali Dal-Badal) expressed his unhappiness over the episode. And, Simranjit Singh Mann, another Akali-faction MP threatened to stage dharna in the Lok Sabha in deference to the wishes of the Deputy speaker. These rumblings in the Akali MPs show that there is more to the sordid story than that meets the eye. In this context, Air Marshall Sekhon's statement that his case is not an isolated one also brings forth the impression that there are quite a few skeletons in the cupboard.

All said and done, it must be admitted that political patronage is an all-pervading phenomenon in almost all the Central Ministries. Though Defence Ministry cannot be singled out and insulated from this infliction altogether, necessary and sufficient care should be taken to avoid any unpleasant and unsavoury situations.

❖❖❖

89. HYPOCRISY

The editorial 'Secular Flag-waving' hits the nail on the head. The hypocrisy of the so-called secular allies of the BJP has been fully exposed and the true colour of each of these parties was brought out in clear-cut terms. They are willing to strike but take care not to wound.

In feet, these parties have made a mockery of secularism. It is doubtful, if any of them can visualize the true meaning of the word and act accordingly. Very few know that it has evolved and originated in England over the ages after painful years of rivalry between the State and the Church. It is concerned only with worldly or temporal affairs and not with those of the sacred or monastic. It is opposed to religious bigotry of the State. It is a rule by monarchs (now democratic leaders), not by monks. In short, it is the belief that the State is divorced from theocracy. The sum and substance of secularism is to keep religion separate from politics and State.

That being the case, it is beyond the comprehension of any thinker, how our parties employ religion as a tool to gain political dividends and still proclaim that they are secular. In the process, they tend to hoodwink the public by holding the banner of secularism with the induction of a few people from the minorities. In this routine (yes, it has become routine for them), they do not perceive the incalculable harm they are inflicting on the secular fabric of the nation. In this context, the edit rightly emphasizes 'secularism is more than just a label to be flaunted in their own interest and at their own convenience'.

❖❖❖

90. POTA

The approval of POTA in a historic joint session of the two Houses of Parliament was preceded by charges and counter-charges by both the Treasury benches and the Opposition. The session has all the trappings of an orchestrated melodrama. In contrast witness the American scenario. Though the US is a vibrant democracy that jealously upholds fundamental human rights, the Bush administration could get the approval of the US Congress for a very stringent anti-terrorism law, which hardly met with any Opposition either from the Republicans or the Democrats. It seems that the September 11 did make difference for the Americans, while the December 13 made no difference at all for us.

Now, whatever be the compulsions of our opposition parties in vehemently opposing the measure, it is incumbent on them to implement the same in the States governed by them. They should realize and remember that all the States, whatever be their political dispensation, are inalienable constituent segments of the Union. The Union laws become, automatically, applicable in all the States without exception.

Then, there is the distinct possibility that provisions of the Act may be used as instruments of repression of the minority communities. It is the sacred duty of the judiciary to see to it that this was not done. In this context, NHRC may play a positive role in ensuring that the basic human rights of minorities are not trampled upon or violated by partisan State Governments like Gujarat. The Union Government has the unenviable responsibility to neutralize both the enemy within and without. In this regard, it is pertinent to emphasize that terrorists have neither religion nor human rights. They should be dealt with as such, under the provisions of the POTA, very sternly.

91. NARAMEDHAM

The Naramedham (genocide) in Gujarat has very few parallels in India's history during the last century. I recall the pre-Partition days when the province of Bengal was united, with Muslims in majority. During 1946, it was governed by the Muslim League under Prime Minister (not chief minister as it is now) Hasan Shahid Suhrawardy. The Muslim League supremo Mohammed Ali Jinnah called upon the Muslims for direct action on August 16, 1946, in order to achieve his dreamland – Pakistan. What followed in Bengal was ruthless murder and mayhem of the minority Hindu community, intensity of riots being the worst in Calcutta and many other places like Naukali. Suhrawardy, like Roman king Nero who played fiddle while Rome was burning, remained a spectator unwilling to control the wretched situation. In exactly a year later, Bengal was divided (of course, with Punjab as well). The country was partitioned while it achieved freedom and Pakistan became a reality.

At present, after a lapse of 55 years, what so far happened and is still happening in Gujarat was just a replica of pre-Partition Bengal. If we replace the Muslim majority Bengal with the Hindu majority Gujarat and H.S. Suhrawardy with the BJP-cum-R.S.S. Pracharak C.M. Narendra Modi, then the ghastly episode would be complete. A partition took place then, much against the wishes of Mahatma

Gandhi, under the aegis of the imperial British. Now, what the BJP and its Sangh Parivar want, by creating an inferno in Gujarat? A second Partition? Alas!, there is no Mahatma Gandhi or Sardar Vallabhbhai Patel to avert it. Albeit, there is a saving grace and silver lining in the evolving darkness, threatening to engulf the country and that is the people of India, as it can be observed that the rest of India is relatively calm in the face of grave provocation emanating from Gujarat. Yes!. The people can save this country from the dark forces of disintegration and disruption.

❖❖❖

92. BABU'S BLUFF

The editorial 'Conscience of Convenience' shows the AP CEO, N. Chandrababu Naidu in a very poor light and takes a dim view of his tactics with respect to the NDA, and BJP in particular. It exhorts that it is time Naidu called off his bluff.

It seems as if he is looking for some concessions from the Centre, whenever he makes some loud noise and tantrums on any particular issue. When the going is not good, he tries to reason out and show some lame excuses to pull out of the unsavoury situation. When he sought Modi's ouster, it is only to assuage the seemingly hurt feelings of Muslim component of TDP, while, at the same time, giving full support to the Hindutwa BJP. He wants to run with the hares and hunt with the hounds, both at a time. All this proves that his secularism is only skin-deep. Even if Naidu were really to withdraw support from the NDA, it will most certainly be, for reasons more hard-nosed than adherence to a principle. No further comment is required on his political strategy.

❖❖❖

93. MLA'S TOUR

The foreign jaunt of a staggering number of MLAs in five batches, ostensibly for a 'study tour' (of five nations) was not taken in by the MEA favourably. Perhaps, they never before countenanced such a bizarre and quixotic proposal from any other State, involving enormous public expenditure, amounting ₹ 4 crore. It is patently an outright fraud on people. But, then, TDP leader Erran Naidu certainly under specific instructions from the TDP supremo, met Prime Minister Vajpayee and got it Okayed. That is, the TDP has extracted its 'pound of flesh' well in advance, before the crucial date. On that day of reckoning, the TDP abstained from voting, much to the chagrin of BJP. It was dishonest and illogical on the part of TDP to do so. It is seen to be on the same side of the political fence as its enemy, the Congress, as it agreed to the Congress demand for the removal of Narendra Modi.

However the Government led by BJP survived the 'no-confidence motion'. In the whole episode, TDP's attitude was a story of drift, sleaze and spin. Now, the TDP will be at its old dubious game with the BJP-led Government, all over again, to extract concessions.

❖❖❖

94. BE CAUTIOUS

It seems that Dr. A.P.J. Abdul Kalam has embroiled himself in an imbroglio on his proposition of nuclear deterrence between India and Pakistan in his very first press conference. He has unwittingly contributed to Gen. Pervez Musharraf's view expressed earlier that Pakistan's Islamic (read Nuclear) bomb prevented India from attacking it. His talk on nuclear weaponry in a flippant manner attracted the attention of Gen. V.P. Malik (Retd.) who opined that acquisition of nuclear weapons by both the countries is no deterrent to war and a limited conventional war is a distinct possibility in the near future.

Dr. Kalam could have easily avoided any inconvenient question from the Press. He should be more circumspect henceforth in airing his views on various matters, in particular when he meets the Press. He should know that, being a presidential nominee, his actions, moves and words are being closely watched by one and all with unabated interest. In view of the same, it would be better if he acquaints himself with national issues of importance including security scenario by experts in respective fields. The edit also brings out this aspect clearly in the concluding.

❖❖❖

95. NATIVE

Announcing the poll schedule for Jammu & Kashmir, CEO J.M. Lyngdoh made a remarkable statement, "There is no question of the Whiteman coming to observe what the native is doing." I would have been happier if he had used the words 'local inhabitant' instead of 'native'. This is because; 'The English' applied with contempt the word 'native' to describe coloured people or non-Europeans. Be it as it may, I consider that Lyngdoh has performed yeoman service by asserting and echoing the sentiments of millions of Indians who never considered themselves as "Whiteman's burden" (this phrase was being used by the British during the heydays of their empire).

Lyngdoh remarks were made in the context of allowing foreign observers to oversee the J&K elections, as desired by the US Secretary of State Gen. Colin Powell. But, the former prime minister I.K. Gujral, while participating in Karan Thaper's 'Line of Fire' programme telecasted on SAB TV, took serious and strong exception to the CEC bringing in the colour issue, stating that Gen. Powell was not a whiteman. This reflects a colonial mindset which is the bane of many an educated in India. Gujral has thoroughly misunderstood the intent and purport of the CEC's remarks. Lyngdoh is certainly not practising 'Apartheid'. He only meant that, nobody's (including the Whiteman's) certificate is required that J&K elections would be free and fair. The Election Commission is indeed capable and efficient of doing so, without the assistance of the Whiteman.

❖❖❖

96. UNITY IN PERIL

Modiism's unparalleled and unprecedented success in Gujarat elections gave the BJP the much-needed vigorous thrust in its electoral fortunes which were at low ebb for quite some time. In contrast, the Congress which was on a winning spree so far, met with its Waterloo in Gujarat. It has, signally, failed to put across aggressively the message of communal harmony, peace and tranquility so absolutely necessary for sustained development of the State. Even so, the quantum of BJP victory is staggering enough to confound all secular and right-thinking Indians. Obviously, the politics of communal passion and hatred implanted in the State's people by the militant groups of the BJP represented by Modi and his cohorts have ruled the roost.

Modiism characterised by hatred and bashing of minorities has come to stay without inhibition. As this was experimented upon and found exceptionally successful in the laboratory called Gujarat, the BJP may now be emboldened to employ the very same malignant and vicious policy with accelerated speed in other states as well to reap rich electoral harvest. It would not bother or worry itself about any constraints or qualms binding on it, by virtue of being a big brother in NDA in implementing its programme of decimation and hate. And so, at least at this juncture, it is the bounden duty of secular parties of all hues to bury their hatchets and form a secular coalition to thwart and defeat the harmful designs of BJP and its fellow-travellers who are intent on tearing asunder the secular fabric of the nation. The coalition so formed has to resuscitate the secular nature of the people throughout the country. Unity is in peril. The secular parties should rise to the occasion and defend it with all their might. Then only, the BJP's ambitious and grandiose designs to convert India into a theocratic state would be contained.

❖❖❖

97. PUNISHMENT

The exemplary capital punishment awarded by the special court judge S.N. Dhingra to the three accused, purportedly involved in criminal conspiracy in the context of Dec 13 attack on Parliament is certainly unexceptionable. This is one of the many sensitive and emotive cases the judiciary has dealt with and disposed of with harsh sentences. Judicial discretion in such cases plays a dominant role in awarding death penalty and there is no proof against the miscarriage of justice under the pressure of surrounding social sentiment and emotion. An example is that of Rajiv Gandhi assassination case. While the designated court pronounced death sentence on a record number of 26 accused, the Supreme Court confirmed the lower court verdict on only four of the lot. This is not to say that judicial verdicts are not punctuated and tinctured with only the merits of the case and law of the land.

As for the case in respect of Parliament, the part played by at least one of the three accused S.A.R. Geelani, the suspended lecturer of Delhi University seems to be minimal in the overall conspiracy. Even if he was found unequivocally guilty, he should have been shown some consideration in view of his respectable position in the university. True, those who wage war against their own country are traitors and deserve no mercy. But, still Geelani seems to be an honourable man, lured by his co-religionists to get himself indirectly involved in the perpetration of the gruesome event. Should he, therefore, deserve some mercy? Yes. It is said that 'Mercy seasons justice and it falls as the gentle rain from heaven, without any strain', thanks to Shakespeare's PORTIA in his comedy "The Merchant of Venice". This did not happen in his case.

98. COMPENSATION

Recently, lawyers all over the country went on strike in defiance of the Supreme Court order announcing it illegal. This might have created law and order problem for the law-enforcement authorities at quite a few places, but was managed by them admirably with least friction. Apart from this aspect, the strike itself should have attracted the provisions of 'contempt of court' law. But, it seems that the Supreme Court has turned a Nelson's eye over the matter, ostensibly to avoid a certain confrontation between the Bench and the Bar. So far, so good.

In addition to the banning of strikes by the legal fraternity, the Supreme Court had also provided for compensation for the clients to obviate their discomfiture due to the absence of lawyers from day-to-day court proceedings. But, the very idea of compensation and its quantification may not be practicable in implementation. Instead, it would, perhaps be more advisable to incorporate a set of measures in the CPC to prevent unscrupulous lawyers from extracting enormous expenses from the gullible clients, thus victimizing them for approaching the court for justice. It is common knowledge that in quite a few civil suits, the fee extracted by a lawyer would abnormally exceed the suit-value itself!

99. SECULARISM

The article 'To Survive, Remain Together' by Kuldip Nayar is well essayed. He says, "Secularism, which we chose despite Partition on the basis of religion, was a settled fact." It suited the diversity of our society. True, but, by incorporating the word 'secularism' in the Constitution, we thought that the Hindu-Muslim question was also settled once and for all. We made no effort to educate people and propagate among them the fundamental features and nuances of secularism. We took it for granted that people are secular by nature. Meanwhile, the Hindutva protagonists made slow but steady progress in dividing people, resulting in communal polarization to some extent, at least in Gujarat.

During the pre-Partition days, Mahatma Gandhi and Pandit Nehru could only pacify the warring Hindus and Muslims in Bengal and Bihar. They could not bridge over the gap between the two communities and so Partition was unavoidable and became a reality. The Partition was a moment of sorrow for Mahatma Gandhi to which he never agreed, as he very well knew that it would not solve the communal problem. True to his thinking, the problem remained as a nagging and hanging fire even after the Muslims secured Pakistan.

At least now, secular parties including Congress and CPM should come together on a common platform and form a united secular front, to thwart the divisive designs of the BJP and its appendages like the VHP to divide and rule. Such a front should also assimilate, imbibe and inculcate the secular values among people by taking recourse to a sustained campaign on unity and secularism, if we have to survive as a nation-state. If we do not pull together, we decimate and perish apart.

❖❖❖

100. CHANGE OF GUARD

The Congress high command effected a change of guard in Maharashtra by imposing S.K. Shinde. Vilasrao Deshmukh was shown the door, because the high command considered him no longer suitable to run the State and lead the Congress to victory in the ensuing State Assembly elections in October 2004. Shinde seems to have been rewarded, being an unsuccessful vice-presidential candidate. Of course, Shinde is essentially a humble and seasoned stalwart of the Congress.

The unceremonious removal of Deshmukh raises a plethora of unsolved problems. First and foremost, the authority, the so-called high command, arrogates to itself to recommend or replace a chief minister, in spite of his good record, is a blatant show of power corrupting itself in a democratic set-up. And, it is rightly said that power corrupts and absolute power corrupts absolutely. This could easily be check-mated by the legislature concerned. Secondly, would it be proper to have more than one chief minister during a five-year term of the Assembly? Certainly not, if continuity of good governance is the norm. A State could easily have a number of corrupt and inefficient chief ministers, if change for its own sake is the norm followed by the high command. Again, who is to remove an incompetent chief minister, in case he commands the goodwill of the high command? In this case, the Assembly could be the arbiter and should be courageous enough to remove the incumbent without submitting to the whims and fancies of the high command, to uphold the democratic values and provide good administration to the people.

❖❖❖

101(a). NETAJI BECAME AN UNSUNG HERO

The birthday of Netaji Subhash Chandra Bose went by on January 23 without anyone taking much notice. During the year 1936, Bose desired to become the president of the Indian National Congress against Mahatma Gandhi's wishes. The Congress Working Committee, with the concurrence of the Mahatma, put up Dr. Bhogaraju Pattabhi Sitaramaiah as its candidate. However, Bose scored a comfortable victory over Pattabhi. The Mahatma then said, "Pattabhi's defeat is my defeat." This shows Bose's popularity rivaled that of the Mahatma's. Regrettably, the present generation has almost forgotten him.

Note: I received a cash prize of ₹ 200 from the Deccan Chronicle management for this letter under the best category.

❖❖❖

101(b). BOSE

The birthday of Netaji Subhash Chandra Bose on January 23 has gone without a whimper. It was, of course, celebrated in West Bengal. It would be informative to recall that during the later-half of the thirties, Bose desired to become the President of Indian National Congress, against the wishes of Mahatma Gandhi. The Congress Working Committee with the concurrence of the Mahatma put up Dr. B. Pattabhi Sitaramaiah as its candidate. An election became inevitable and ultimately, Bose won over Pattabhi with a comfortable majority. It was on record that the Mahatma admitted the discomfiture saying 'Pattabhi's defeat is my defeat'. This shows the immense popularity of Bose in those years, surpassing even that of the Mahatma, but, it is regrettable that the present generation has almost forgotten him.

❖❖❖

102. GILANI'S ARREST

The arrest of Syed Iftikar Gilani, chief of New Delhi Bureau of Jammu-based 'Kashmir Times' under the provisions of Official Secrets Act and his subsequent release after seven months proved to be a fiasco. However, in the first place, the Government cannot be faulted upon when it put him behind the bars, under the impression that the document found with him is a sensitive one. The very same document said to be crucial by the investigating agencies was published in a Pakistan journal and readily available on Internet. Then only, it was evaluated and found by the military intelligence officials that it was of 'negligible security value'. The government could have immediately ordered his unconditional release. And this was not done, casting a shadow on the efficacy and efficiency of both the executive and judiciary. This episode should make our intelligence agencies more circumspect than ever before. Even so, they should not develop clay feet and slip into inaction. They should be ever vigilant to thwart the evil designs of our recalcitrant western neighbour. The internal surveillance should continue with unmitigated rigour and vigour.

❖❖❖

103. COMMUNISTS

The edit 'How many heroes left' has come not a day too soon. It is castigating, scathing and stinging in its criticism of Indian Communists. It is highly appropriate and has the nail on the head. In this context, I recall the former President (Late) Neelam Sanjeeva Reddy's sarcastic comment: "CPI is the Russian Party and CPM is the Chinese Party. So, where is the Indian Communist Party?" Only after the Soviet Union split and China opted for a diluted market economy, our Communists have started Indianising themselves and their theories. They have begun admitting their blunders and failures. Buddhadev Bhattacharjee's apology for the mistake and unholy estimate of Netaji falls in this category.

The uncharitable remarks in the edit on Karl Marx, admittedly one of the greatest social thinkers of yore, are far removed from historicity. His 'surplus-value' theory is still relevant and valid. Even in these times of welfare states, the workers are not paid equal to their work input and the unpaid value of their work forms the surplus-value; this value is being appropriated by the bourgeoisie and capitalists, in addition to the profits they accrue on the product output. The result is that the rich are becoming richer and the poor, poorer. So, it can be said that Karl Marx theory is timeless and universal. Age cannot wither nor custom stale its infinite variety, as William Shakespeare remarked on the unquestionable beauty of

'CLEOPATRA', the Queen of Egypt, in his famous play "ANTONY AND CLEOPATRA".

❖❖❖

104(a). GIVE SAVARKAR HIS DUE

Vinayak Damodar Savarkar is a much maligned person. Very few realise that he believed in an united India, even during his student days. He was the first college student in British India to be rusticated for treason. Savarkar authored a fiery history and literary work titled 'The Indian War of Independence – 1857' on Sepoy Mutiny against the British rule in that year. It was banned by the British out of fear that it would incite people to rebellion. It is sad that people judge him only on the basis of his alleged involvement in Gandhiji's murder, forgetting his other contributions.

❖❖❖

104(b). SAVARKAR ROW

The unveiling of Vinayak Damodar Savarkar's portrait in the Central Hall of Parliament stirred a Hornets' nest and has become a subject of controversy. It is unfortunate that his memorable role in the freedom struggle was sought to be denigrated. As a student in London, he dreamt of an united India. Very few knew that he was the first student to be rusticated in UK for treason. He escaped from the clutches of the British and swam the English Channel to reach the French coast and to freedom. It earned him the epithet "Veer". The French, however, did not appreciate his zeal for freedom and colluded with the British to hand him over to them who subsequently sent him to the cellular jail in Andamans to be tortured.

He authored a treatise on the Sepoy Mutiny titled 'The Indian War of Independence – 1857', by accessing information and records from the 'India Office Library' in London. The book was promptly banned in British India. By this work, he earned an immortal fame as an articulate and fiery patriot.

❖❖❖

105. RACISM

Cricketers Henry Olanga and his team-mate Andy Flower wore black arm-bands in their teams' World Cup League match in Harare, 'to mourn the death of democracy' in their homeland Zimbabwe.

They protested symbolically against the dictatorial attitude of their President Robert Mugabe. But, fearing retribution, they have opted to settle elsewhere, most probably in England or Australia. This is a pointer to Mugabe's ruthlessness.

Mugabe has violated all the democratic norms. He launched a violent campaign to drive away many a White farmer from their hearths and homes. Earlier, when Rhodesia, the present Zimbabwe, was ruled by the White minority, the Whites practiced apartheid harassing the Blacks in all possible ways. This practice was condemned by the world community.

Now, Mugabe is practicing the same policy of apartheid against the Whites. But no Government except the US and a few in Europe censured the Mugabe government for its anti-White policies. French President Jacques Chirac even rolled out a red carpet for him. It is time that all democratic governments condemn Mugabe's unholy policies and practices.

106. KASHMIRIYAT

Terrorists have mowed down innocent Pandits at Nadimarg in South Kashmir. It is nothing short of systematic genocide. Pathetic as it is, it points to grave ramifications. The elimination of Pandits, still remaining in Kashmir, seems to be the emerging scenario.

Of equal ferocity were the killings of Sikhs at Chattisinghpur, some three years ago. Again, much earlier than this, quite a few persons of a community were gunned down at Doda. These murders most foul indicate that Kashmir has become a gallery of horrors.

There is a method and a pattern noticeable in all these wanton massacres, by the terrorists aided and abetted by Pakistan. They aim to send out all the minorities from the Kashmir Valley. In fact, this was what was done in Pakistan, in the aftermath of partition in 1947.

Such an 'ethnic cleansing' as it is called now, converts Kashmir into a home for Muslims and only Muslims, similar to that of Pakistan. It imparts a body blow to the very ethos of Kashmiriyat, the secular identity of Kashmir with a long history. And, it is regrettable that the Government, with all its paramilitary and military forces, working in tandem, could not prevent the recurrence of such diabolical and heinous criminal events.

❖❖❖

107. PARTITION OF INDIA WAS INEVITABLE

The recent articles by Dr. Rafiq Zakaria and Balbir K. Punz repeat the history of the Hindu-Muslim issue as viewed by each of them. In particular, the latter's version is biased and skewed. Even without a Savarkar or a Jinnah, the British would have partitioned India. Even Mahatma Gandhi could not prevent it. As regards tl takeover of the secular Congress after the British, there is much adu about nothing in Punj's essay. The Congress was responsible for democracy taking strong roots in this country and bringing a sense of belonging among the Muslims in India, in the days when the BJP or its variants were not even around.

❖❖❖

108. YSR YATRA

Congress Legislature Party leader Y.S. Rajasekhara Reddy began his 'padayatra' or pilgrimage in mid-summer by risking his own health. He was actually held up for a week at the outskirts of Rajahmundry due to sunstroke. He could have easily taken up a helicopter-yatra or aircraft yatra. But, he did not opt for it, as he wanted to identify himself with the commoners, who travelled by walking or at the most by bullock cart.

He wanted to acquaint and associate himself with the people's aspirations, trials and tribulations. In pursuit of the same, wherever he went, people met him in large numbers and explained theii problems to him.

Padayatras are not new to Congress. Mahatma Gandhi walked all the way from Sabarmati Ashram to the sea-side village of Dandi in Gujarat to pick a fistful of salt, in protest against the salt tax imposed by the Britishers. This was known as salt satyagraha.

It is to YSR's credit that he chose to follow this tradition of walking to reach out to the toiling millions. And, by all accounts, his "Praja Prasthanam" seems to be overwhelmingly successful. This may or may not help the Congress at the hustings but he has endeared himself to the poor and the down-trodden.

❖❖❖

109. FIGHTING SOMEONE ELSE'S WAR

The United States intervention in Iraq is prompted by the desire to own Iraqi oil fields and his gemonistic imperial ambitions. So far, there was neither an armistice with the Iraqi generals nor a general amnesty declared. In these circumstances, sending Indian troops to assist US-led and US-commanded occupation forces in Iraq is outrageous.

It implies that we are endorsing the US aggression. If it is to get a few reconstruction contracts in Iraq, then it would be un-Indian and undignified for India becoming a sub-contractor to Pentagon. It will earn us the dubious distinction of a client-state or a satrap of the United States.

Getting involved in this murky enterprise would involve unnecessary expenditure to be incurred by the tax-payer. We would also be inviting the wrath of the Iraqi people who are ill-at-ease with the American dispensation.

It is nobody's case that we automatically curry American favour to get anything substantial in return, except a "Thank you" from the White House. It is fool-hardy to expect the US to make any radical changes in its Pak-centric policy, to get a few battalions of Indian troops to Iraq. It would be a historic blunder to commit our troops to Iraq, subjecting them to the risk of involvement in somebody else's game plan.

❖❖❖

110. LET DOWN BY CHARACTER OR TRADITION?

I refer to the editorial page article 'A Monument for Blunders?' by Balbir K. Punz. I agree with the author that the Hindu character is a harmonious mixture of chivalry and generosity. They follow the dictum: 'Magnanimity in victory and fortitude in adversity'.

Facts are facts; it is a historical truth that Jawaharlal Nehru committed grievous errors in respect of both Kashmir and Tibet. Referring Kashmir to the UN actually negated the solemnisation of its accession to India. But for this folly, our troops would have, in all probability, evicted the invading Pakistani marauders from Kashmir. As regards Tibet, he made avoidable mistakes in gauging Chinese imperial ambitions and taking corrective measures. It resulted in the annexation of Tibet by China in 1950s.

And again, a victorious Indira Gandhi in the 1971 Indo-Pak war, was magnanimous enough to release 93000 Pakistani POWs, without demanding the merger of Pak-occupied Kashmir into India. She did not implement the dictum: 'Victor takes all, but vanquished none', out of misplaced generosity towards Pakistan. Even so, she unwittingly altered the 'balance of power' structure in the sub-continent with the creation of Bangladesh. In the final analysis, it may be said that both Nehru and Indira reflected the Hindu character in ample measure, by committing monumental blunders.

❖❖❖

111. BEIJING DECLARATION

The euphoria generated by the media using sonorous phrases on Beijing declaration and Memorandum of Understanding (MOU) for expansion of trade between India and China seems to be unwarranted. China stood firm on both Tibet and Sikkim and secured what it desired. The centerpiece of the declaration was India's recognition of Tibet Autonomous Region (TAR) as part of China, for the first time in writing, as the Chinese averred. Our reiteration of Tibet's status, without obtaining in return, China's formal recognition of the 1975-merger of Sikkim state into Indian Union may be termed as a virtual sell-out to China. This is particularly so, because in the Chinese maps of India, large tracts of Indian territory in and to the south of Himalayan ranges is shown to be part of China.

Over and above, the MOU-Border Trade agreement as per the Chinese, envisages the opening of the old silk route through 'Nathu La' pass for trade. It could, as well, be used by the Chinese to infiltrate into Sikkim. This is a strategic mistake which could cost us dearly in the long run. It is certainly a win-win situation for China, authored by our magnanimous Prime Minister A.B. Vajpayee. The Indian tiger is crouching instead of poaching. There is every danger of the hidden Chinese dragon devouring the Indian tiger.

❖❖❖

112. HISTORIC AND MOMENTOUS DECISION

After an abnormal prevarication and vacillation, the Vajpayee Government took a historic decision against sending Indian troops to the strife-torn Iraq, without an explicit UN mandate. A hurried and quick deployment of Indian Army personnel in a war-ravaged and half-starved Iraq, as part of the Anglo-American force would have certainly impaired India's unblemished image in Iraq and West Asia as well. It is in tune with, the mood of the intelligentsia and fourth-estate, and honours the public opinion. The Government deserves to be commended on its wise decision, in conformity with our national interests.

Though the US is rueful of our decision, it is to its credit and sagacity that it still considers India as its strategic partner. India, on its part, should consider channelizing its efforts in conjunction with France, Germany and Russia to exert incessant pressure on the Bush-Blair combine to entrust to the UN, the reconstruction work in Iraq reeling under prolonged and unjust sanctions, and a devastating war.

❖❖❖

113. NON-NATO ALLY

US Secretary of State Colin Powell's announcement, in Islamabad that Pakistan could be designated as a 'Non-NATO ally' should surprise nobody including, the Indians.

The US has always considered Pakistan and not India, as its 'front-line state' with a few interregnums now and then. This policy serves the American interests.

After the World War II, the US took over from the British, their position and status as an imperial and hegemonistic power. Hence, Pakistan is being used by the US as a pawn in its power-game.

The US has rewarded Pakistan with the new status, for its offensive (with 70,000-strong troops) against the Talibans and Al-Quida terrorists entrenched in the tribal areas to the east of Durand line between Pakistan and Afghanistan.

In conformity with its new status, Pakistan may receive more sophisticated and advanced weapon systems from the US.

The 'feel-good' factor and hype about a 'strategic partnership' between India and US stands deflated, due to the US indifference in not taking India into confidence over the new status, accorded to Pakistan.

It would be wise on our part to revise our Pakistan-centric policy in the conduct of relations with other nations including the US.

As a mature nation, India needs to safeguard its interests independently, on its own.

❖❖❖

114. SANCTION PUCCA BUILDING FOR ZP SCHOOL

Five decades old Andhra Kesari Tanguturi Prakasam Zilla Parishad High School at Tanuku is devoid of basic infrastructural facilities. The school has a student strength of around 500 and staff of 20. As it has no own building, classes are being run in a rented house in old town. The rooms are not spacious enough to provide for proper seating arrangements for the students. The students are made to sit in cramped rooms without proper air circulation. There is only one toilet both for the pupils and staff members and no separate toilet for girls. There is no laboratory for conducting experiments, no library for general reading and no play-ground.

But the students of the school do not allow the lack of facilities to affect their academic performance as can be seen from the pass percentages achieved by the school in Class VII and SSC examination all these years since its inception.

I appeal to the Zilla Parishad authorities to take measures to sanction a pucca building to the school and provide all the required facilities.

❖❖❖

115. STIR FOR TELANGANA

Nothing has ever been achieved so far in India without agitation, coupled with sacrifice. India has achieved its freedom from foreign yoke in 1947, mainly through Mahatma Gandhi's non-violent, non-cooperation movements and sacrifice of numerous precious lives, though there were also other crucial factors.

Circumstances in the aftermath of the World War II (1939-45) also prompted the British to liquidate their Indian empire. Again, the first-ever linguistic state 'Andhra' was carved out in 1953 from the erstwhile Madras Presidency, due to the supreme sacrifice by Potti Sriramulu.

Coming to the question of Telangana, the demand for its separation from Andhra Pradesh seems to be outlandish and hard to achieve. In fact, in 1969, a violent agitation for the same, spearheaded by Dr. M. Channa Reddy, had fizzled out due to rank insincerity and opportunism of its leaders. Now, a year ago, quite a few disgruntled leaders formed the Telangana Rashtra Samithi under the leadership of K. Chandrasekhara Rao with the sole objective of achieving a separate Telangana state. They chose electoral politics to fructify their demand without resorting to agitation methods. But, the history of Gandhian era and independent India goes against their methods for separation, as people's aspirations have never been realized through electoral means.

❖❖❖

116. UNWARRANTED

In protest against the Chief Justice's notice to two judges of the Punjab and Haryana High Court regarding their honorary membership of a club, 25 judges have chosen to go on leave *en masse*. The judges' reaction is unwarranted.

A strike-like situation in the High Court lowers the dignity of the judges. Their action violates the universally accepted values of judicial conduct. Their unprecedented conduct proves that even the judicial fraternity is not immune to the negative trends in the society. It shows them in poor light. Their action is also in contravention of the Supreme Court ruling that 'to strike work is unconstitutional'. Should the ruling apply only to the working class? All said and done, it seems that a fool-proof methodology to suitably address the issue of judicial accountability is an absolute necessity.

❖❖❖

117. NEXT CM

The electronic and print media are passing sarcastic remarks over speculations in the Congress circles regarding the would-be Chief Minister of Andhra Pradesh. Dissent and contest are the twin corner-stones of the edifice of democracy. Congress Party, since its inception in 1885, followed these conceptual essentials of democracy in form and spirit.

Way back in the latter half of 1930s, Subhash Chandra Bose contested and won the top slot of Congress President against Dr. B. Pattabhi Sitaramaiah, the nominee of Mahatma Gandhi.

Again, when the time came for the selection of Prime Minister of India in 1946-47, Jawaharlal Nehru, Vallabhbhai Patel and J.B. Kripalani were in the race. But, Gandhi's choice of Nehru was accepted by the other two. In 1964, Lal Bahadur Shastri won the contest against Morarji R. Desai for the leadership of Congress to become the Prime Minister. In 1966, the contest between Indira Gandhi and Morarji Desai went in favour of Indira, catapulting her to the coveted job.

It is quite another matter that a few Congress leaders are in unseemly haste and hurry to contest for the CM's post even before the Assembly election results are declared.

❖❖❖

118. INCUMBENCY FACTOR

It was assumed that anti-incumbency factor played a major role in dislodging a government. Incumbency means tenure of a person or a party holding an office, according to the Oxford Dictionary. Hence, the anti-incumbency factor implies the tendency of the people to remove a person or party, on completion of respective tenures, irrespective of their performances in positions of power. This could be one of the reasons, supplementary in nature, but not the sole reason. Our voters could have acquired such an attribute, during the centuries of tortuous subjugation under foreign yoke.

Viewed objectively in this perspective, it may be reasoned out that people below the poverty line and the middle class determine the suitability of the ruling party to govern them and hence its fate as well, during the elections. It is not automatic removal, as some kind of thought process goes behind their decisions, either positive or negative. They assess and estimate the success or failure of the policies of the incumbent in terms of the benefits percolated to them. As is always the case, the economic conditions of the commoners and the middle class did not change for the better in the present context also, due to the unimaginative policies and reforms implemented by a few State Governments and the Central Government with Platonic fervour. The results of the recent elections testify to the people's anguish and disgust over the ruling parties' on-performance and not to their incumbency.

❖❖❖

119. MAHATMA BY CHANCE

Sonia Gandhi's abdication of power has been variously interpreted by many persons of eminence, the Fourth Estate and the electronic media. These interpretations are bordered on sycophancy.

Some called her as a Mahatma, as she said she was guided by her "inner voice" while making her decision, only to camouflage and hide her real intentions and motives. In this context, they used superlative epithets like 'sacrifice' and 'renunciation' conveniently forgetting the fact that she is no saint. It seems she abjured power only to assume the same at an appropriate and propitious time later.

Had she secured her party a comfortable majority in Lok Sabha instead of a meagre 145 seats, she would, in all probability, never have opted out. Had she eschewed power, she would never have retained the post of Congress Parliamentary Party chairperson. By relinquishing the top slot and offering the same to Dr. Manmohan Singh, she achieved four political objectives, namely: (a) becomes more popular with the Congress workers and MPs, (b) suppresses her foreign origin issue for the time being, thus leaving BJP and its cohorts with no emotive and tangible point-of-fact, for agitation, (c) gets accolades for the selection of an outstanding person of proven capabilities and unblemished character for the premiership and (d) creates a halo around herself by her scheming and shrewd sacrifice. And, with all these positives in her basket, she could easily become a remote control over the incumbent Prime Minister, to get things done the way she wants.

She appears to be an astute and a tactful political player, with none to match her abilities in her party circle.

❖❖❖

120. EU EXPANSION

What began as an ECM (European Common Market) with Germany and France as its prominent members, has graduated into a ten-member European Union (EU) with a common Parliament and with 'EURO' as its common currency.

With the inclusion of an ensemble of eight erstwhile Communist States including Poland and Hungary and Mediterranean islands Malta and a divided Cyprus, the EU has become a powerful but loose confederation of 25 states with 450 million people, that could match the US economic and political clout.

The EU cannot be a mere appendage of the US. It could thwart the US imperial ambitions too. So, the emergence of EU as a balancing force in the international relations could be a matter of interest to the Asia-Pacific region, including India. This region has witnessed the emergence of economic groupings like ASEAN and SAARC in the last few decades. Each of these groupings may get an impetus to further strengthen its economic bonding by evolving a common currency, following the analogy and example of the EU.

In the immediate present, the enlarged EU provides ample and varied opportunities for India. Before its expansion, the EU was India's largest trading partner. Now, India could develop its trade manifold with the new members of EU to make its developing economy a flourishing and vibrant one.

❖❖❖

121. INDIAN DIARCHY

We heard of 'diarchy' during the British East India Company's reign in Bengal. Diarchy means a form of government in which two persons, states or bodies are jointly vested with supreme powers. It implies governance by dual power centres. Such a system of government took shape during the rule of Robert Clive. He became the governor of Bengal, consequent upon his surprise victory in the battle of Plassey in 1757. The Company used to collect the revenue while the Nawab of Bengal was provided with residual powers of administration. This kind of arrangement led to diarchy. It was institutionalized during the regime of Governor General Warren Hastings, through the 'Regulating Act' in 1773.

Due to the inherent cross-currents in governance, it was later abolished, investing unfettered powers in the office of the Governor-General. However, it was again ushered in 1920s under Montague-Chelmsford Reforms.

That was all during the British hegemony over India, but now, in independent India, it seems that 'the vestiges of colonial rule' have again surfaced with renewed vigour. We are witnessing the emergence of two power centres which lead to duality in governance.

Under the aegis of Congress, Sonia Gandhi, has become a supreme power head, what with investing herself with the offices of chairperson of the Congress Parliamentary Party, the United Progressive Alliance and that of the National Advisory Council. Prime Minister Manmohan Singh and his Cabinet colleagues are her nominees only. But even so, the prerogatives vested in his position may eventually make him turn around in defiance, questioning the overall supervisory authority and status of Sonia Gandhi.

Slowly but steadily, they could develop into dual power houses working at cross-purposes to the detriment of the national interests.

❖❖❖

122. GHASTLY INCIDENT

Words fail to fathom the tragedy that struck MCA final year student Revuri Srilakshmi. Her killing by her class fellow Y. Manohar in Vijayawada was shocking. The newspaper heading 'Murder Most Foul' drawn from Shakespeare's 'Macbeth' was appropriate. Ambitious Macbeth killed his guest King Duncan in sleep to become the king. But in this case, there was no reason except the perpetrator's lust, prejudice and sadism.

A number of newspapers showed the concerned college management in poor light. The delay in shifting the bleeding Srilakshmi to a hospital was intriguing. The college authorities' explanations before the two-member committee of the National Commission for Women were far from convincing.

Even the three-member inquiry committee of Nagarjuna University found the college wanting on several counts. It was astounding how the college administration admitted a person of dubious character into the post-graduate class.

Neither the police nor the college management did cover themselves with glory for their lethargy in initiating corrective action when the matter was brought to their notice by the aggrieved girl much in advance of the deadly assault on her.

❖❖❖

123. LOW INTEREST RATES CRIPPLE

The low-interest regime followed by the government and the RBI has been crippling the poor and middle class. The UPA Budget presented by P. Chidambaram provides some comfort to senior citizens, as it gives them a return of nine per cent interest on their savings. Other low-income groups are left high and dry. Savings deposits are said to be maintained solely in the depositors' interests. But low interest rates of nationalized banks discourage people from depositing their money in these banks. In fact, pensioners and persons completely dependent on the interest accrued on their savings are the worst hit. So, it is imperative that the RBI progressively increase the interest rate. This will help meet the social security and social justice objectives of the government.

❖❖❖

124. FALLING 'INTEREST'

The interest rates offered by the State Bank of India and other nationalized banks on savings schemes including fixed time deposits are too meagre (about 5 to 6 per cent) to promote savings among the people. Post offices also offer a number of savings schemes providing better interest rates than those of banks. These deposits are maintained solely in the depositors' interest. The low interest rates do not encourage people to invest their hard-earned money either in the banks or in the post offices. If some people are still investing in them, it is only for safety reasons. The most important factor that encourages the middle classes to save part of their income is to multiply their savings over a period by investing it in fixed time deposits. The aim is to draw their money later with the accrued interest for utilizing the same for their progeny's education or marriage, or for their sustenance in their twilight years. However, the prevalent interest rates do not encourage them. Out of sheer necessity, they are compelled to approach private money lenders for loans at abnormal rates of interest (more than 24 per cent per annum). The situation will, in turn, make them miserable in the evenings of their lives, if they fail to clear their debts. Hence, the very purpose of the banks or post offices to protect the interests of depositors would be defeated. Pensioners, senior citizens and persons wholly dependent on the interest accrued on their savings and deposits for their survival, are the worst hit by the existing interest regime. And, social security of these people is in doldrums. In fact, small income groups are driven to serfdom by the unimaginative policies of the government and the Reserve Bank of India in progressively decreasing the interest rates on small savings, including fixed deposits.

❖❖❖

125. GOVERNOR'S SACK

The cardinal principle of justice from the days of Magna-Carta is that no person shall be punished except by the due process of law. This dictum was set aside before dismissing the Governors by the Congress-led government at the Centre. This single act of the Government has tarnished the credibility and respectability of the office of the Governor. No government at the Centre in the past few decades had protected the honour and dignity of the Governor's office. Eventually, the Governor's office, selection of suitable person to this office and removal of the incumbent have become a bone of contention between the Opposition and the treasury benches. During the days of Nehru, the appointees to the gubernatorial posts brought credence to their office. Subsequently, the post became a rehabilitation centre for power-crazy politicians who lost electoral battles. The very goal of creation of this post by the founders of the Constitution was defeated by the whims and fancies of successive governments. In addition to these, the institution of Governors also entails huge expenditure on the exchequer. It is an anachronism and a vestige of foreign yoke! Now atleast, the Congress-led coalition government at the center should redeem its pledge to abolish the institution of governors, instead of denigrating it. Alternatively, the governor could be elected by the people, as is the case in United States. The governor would then, be in the office in his own right.

❖❖❖

126. SEPARATE ANDHRA

Telangana is getting the lion's share in almost all spheres, including ministerial berths both at the Centre and in the State. Rayalaseema follows suit. But coastal Andhra region is nowhere in the reckoning. Legitimate interests of Andhra area have been overlooked. After the formation of Andhra Pradesh in 1956, the coastal region has gained nothing development-wise. But the growth in certain fields like education, industries and health-care was phenomenal in parts of Telangana, including the twin cities.

Successive governments of Andhra Pradesh did precious little to develop even the backward areas like north coastal districts and the

Palnadu area in Guntur district. Sir Arthur Cotton, during the British Raj, was responsible for the construction of dams across rivers Godavari and Krishna, which turned the delta fertile. There was no further development in coastal districts, since Independence. So, there exists a strong case to carve out a separate Andhra state with the nine coastal districts before forming a separate Telangana state.

❖❖❖

127. TAINTED MINISTERS

Jharkhand Mukthi Morcha supremo Shibu Soren's unedifying episode while he was in the Cabinet did hardly any credit to the Congress-led United Progressive Alliance government. Close on its heels, another inglorious episode involving Telangana Rashtra Samithi leader and Cabinet Minister, K. Chandrasekhara Rao on charges of cheating and breach of trust appears to be in the offing. Prime Minister Manmohan Singh seems to be unconcerned with the goings-on in his ministry.

As it is, there are quite a few corrupt ministers in his Cabinet. And he blames it, quite conveniently, on the coalition compulsions. Any representative Government must be beyond reproach.

It is no argument to say that since BJP-led National Democratic Alliance government had a few tainted ministers when they were in power, the Congress-led coalition also could have some tainted ministers.

The coalition partners could, by mutual consultation and agreement, induct persons of unblemished record and integrity into the Cabinet.

In fact, both the Congress and the BJP are the obverse and reverse sides of the same coin. One tries to malign or obfuscate the other.

Congress swears by secularism and goes on appeasing the Muslims. BJP also swears by true secularism or Hindu nationalism called Hindutva, promising to treat all sections of the society equally well, with no appeasement to any particular section. It seems the two-some are tweedledum and tweedledee differing only in name.

❖❖❖

128. SEPARATE ANDHRA

Telangana is getting the lion's share in almost all spheres including ministries at the State and the national level. Rayalaseema too has had its share. But it is the coastal region whose interests have been overlooked.

In fact, the coastal regions had gained nothing after the formation of the State in 1956. Whatever development took place was in Telangana.

Growth in certain fields like education, industries and healthcare was phenomenal in parts of Telangana, including the twin cities. Successive Governments did precious little to develop backward areas like north coastal districts and Palnadu in Guntur district.

Sir Arthur Cotton during the British regime was responsible for the construction of the dams across Godavari and Krishna, which made the delta areas fertile. There was no further development in coastal districts since independence. And so there exists a strong case to carve out a separate Andhra with the nine coastal districts rather the formation of a separate Telangana.

❖❖❖

129. FUEL PRICE HIKE

Successive governments at the Centre went on progressively increasing the prices of petrol and diesel. The present government also thought it prudent to raise the already exorbitant prices of petrol and diesel. These fuel oils are essential for the transportation of various commodities and goods by road and rail. They also serve as fuel to heavy duty as well as light motor vehicles. Hence, a raise in fuel prices would lead to a chain reaction, leading to a corresponding nightmarish increase of almost every commodity and transport systems. It is essentially a question of who bears the burden of oil shock and in what proportion it is distributed. The sharing has to be done mainly by commuters and consumers, the government and oil companies. The increase of oil prices at present, would lead corresponding price increase in all essential commodities, goods and services. Consequently, the middle class and the poor have to bear the brunt of the upward surge of prices of transportation and essential articles. And it will cut into the meagre finances of these sections of the society.

Oil prices are being increased in tune with the prevailing global oil price system. But, the standard of living of the people in this country has not gone up to the level of international standards. Hence, the increase is not at all justified. The government would be advised to review its upward revision of fuel prices. However, if the increase in fuel oils is unavoidable, then the government should reduce the costs of services so that price level of essential commodities is kept reasonably low.

❖❖❖

130. EC MISSIVE

Four elements have put our democracy in peril. They are corruption, criminalization, electoral malpractice and nepotism. The Election Commission's recent missive to the Congress-led UPA government on barring persons with criminal antecedents from entering the portals of legislature is remarkable.

There is nothing wrong in preventing persons convicted by courts or persons found guilty of abuse of power by commissions of inquiry, from participating in the electoral processes. The principle of criminal justice that a person could be treated innocent unless and until he was proved guilty, should not be made applicable in such cases.

We at present, witness a spectacle of unworthy persons of questionable disposition, occupying the treasury benches in Parliament.

Such a sorry situation would not have come to pass had they been disallowed to partake in electoral contests. A way out has to be evolved to eject such unholy elements of tarnished character from our polity.

❖❖❖

131. SPLIT AP INTO 3?

Andhra University which was established at Bezawada (now Vijayawada) in 1926 was shifted to Visakhapatnam by the then Vice-chancellor C.R. Reddy. The shifting by Dr. Reddy to the seaside Waltair was necessitated due to the unbearable summer heat of the town, nick-named by him as Blazewada.

Consequently, the four districts of Rayalaseema opted to get affiliated to Madras University, as they felt that Waltair was far away from them. To keep them united with the nine coastal districts to form an Andhra State, "Sri Bagh Pact" was concluded at Madras under the aegis of coastal leaders doctor B. Pattabhi Sitaramaiah, Tanguturi Prakasam Pantulu and others. Now, as per newspaper reports, some Rayalaseema leaders have proposed to the Congress leadership that if a separate Telangana has to be formed, then a separate Rayalaseema may also be carved out with six districts including the coastal districts of Prakasam and Nellore, ostensibly for the economic viability of the new state. The proposition would not be agreeable to coastal Andhra, as it jeopardizes their interests.

In case, such a denouement takes place as per their demand, the coastal Andhra, should be compensated with the addition of Khammam and Nalgonda districts to it, to make up for the loss of Prakasam and Nellore districts.

In fact, the three regions—Andhra, Rayalaseema and Telangana—are mutually interdependent. If a division of Andhra Pradesh has to be made due to political intrigues, then it should be along the lines of the districts, traditionally included in the three regions and not otherwise.

❖❖❖

132. DROUGHT IN DELTA

The rainfall in the state for the past few years was inadequate leading to drought in some parts of the state including Krishna delta. A solution has to be evolved on why the rainfall is unusually subnormal during the successive years.

Atmospheric heat due to abnormal emission of 'Green house gases', like carbon dioxide (CO_2) and methane (CH_4) could be one of the main reasons for scant rainfall. It is well known that oceans influence weather conditions on the land. In respect of Asian continent, its weather changes are largely influenced by the warming (called El Nino) and cooling (known as La Nina) of the Pacific Ocean. Recent excessive heat conditions experienced in the State might be due to the warming of the Pacific. Seasonal rains are also few and far between in the state.

If the scenario continues to prevail in the coming years, then the rains will dwindle leading to severe scarcity of water. Air and water are the two main life-supporting systems. Air has already been polluted enough. If water availability is also on the wane, the seriousness of the situation can well be imagined. Mostly, weather forecasts go haywire. There is no tangible evidence that concerned organizations are performing any worthwhile study on the subject. It is, therefore, imperative that an atmospheric study group with eminent scientists in the field be constituted by the Government to carry out in-depth studies and investigate the climatic fluctuations and corresponding repercussions and suggest remedial measures to the same for the benefit of the people.

❖❖❖

133. SEPARATE RAYALASEEMA

It is learnt from newspaper reports that some Rayalaseema leaders have proposed to the Congress high command that if a separate Telangana has to be formed, then a separate Rayalaseema may also be carved out with six districts including coastal districts of Prakasam and Nellore, ostensibly for the economic viability of the new State.

This would not be agreeable to coastal Andhra as it jeopardizes their interests. In case, such a denouement takes place, then coastal Andhra should be compensated with the addition of Khammam and Nalgonda districts to it. In fact, the three regions of coastal Andhra, Rayalaseema and Telangana are mutually inter-dependent and their separation would be an ill-advised move. However, if a division of the State due to political intrigues is inevitable, then it must be strictly along the lines of the districts traditionally included in the three regions and not otherwise.

❖❖❖

134. CALCULATED MOVE

Reservations have been enshrined in the Constitution to elevate economically deprived classes on a par with the privileged classes.

This provision has been thoroughly misused by successive governments to reap electoral dividends. It has resulted in social stratification on the basis of caste, class and religion.

In continuation of the tradition, the UPA Government has recently constituted a commission to go into the question of reservations for religious and linguistic minorities. Earlier, the Andhra Pradesh Government's missive providing 5 per cent reservation to Muslims in education and employment sectors, though struck off by the High Court, followed in the same trend. It is certainly a retrograde measure.

It is a calculated move to garner votes of these groups in the ensuing elections in Maharashtra and other states.

Religion and language cannot and could not be the benchmark for reservations. Widening the scope of reservations every now and then is detrimental to the society and national interests. It segments various groups in watertight compartments. It eventually leads to the negation of the motto "unity in diversity", so assiduously cultivated by Jawaharlal Nehru and other illustrious intellectuals and savants of the society. In turn, we will be left only with diversity, unity lying in a shambles.

❖❖❖

135. BEYOND THE REALM OF SCIENCE

Apropos the news item 'Can Prayer Actually Heal?' (TNIE, Oct. 11), studies are being conducted by a few US scientists of prestigious universities like Columbia, Harvard and Washington. The US Federal Government is funding these prayer research projects. So far, they have found that there is every likelihood of women having fertility treatment and being prayed by Christian groups in their interest to have successful pregnancy. This is not the case with women who have not been prayed for. However, the efficacy of prayer in curing human diseases is yet to be established.

This reminds me of the celebrated English poet Tennyson's lines of poetic beauty — "More things are wrought by prayer than these world dreams of" in his epic 'King Arthur and his Knights'.

There is no doubt that prayer bestows undivided concentration of mind and freedom from the surroundings on those who perform it. Their attention is diverted from their bodily ailments, thus providing them solace. It is said that our hermits and sages have realized the primacy of prayer in raising man to ethereal heights from the earthly confines. This is certainly beyond the realm of science and logic.

❖❖❖

136. PRO-RICH GOVERNMENT

The erstwhile NDA government did give the impression of being pro-rich, substantiated by its unimaginative economic policies. Now, the present UPA government, enjoying the outward support of the Communists is also faring no better. Actually, the change of guard has made no perceptible difference to the pro-rich trend of the economy. It seems that any government, by definition favours the rich and the well-to-do as against the poor and the downtrodden.

There can be no comparison between the opulent lifestyle of employees working in multinational corporations and NRI companies with that of the less fortunate ones in the government and private sector. Invariably, the Central Government of whatever party or coalition, turned a Nelson's eye to this anomalous aspect. Every government has worked enthusiastically to make things better for the so-called shining brigade. It conveniently overlooked that a considerable majority in the country has to struggle to eke out a bare existence.

The UPA government professes that it would continue the reforms with a human face. In practice, this is not found to be true. It would seem that the CMP (Common Minimum Programme) is only a suitable camouflage to hide their real intentions.

❖❖❖

137. FAREWELL TO ARMS

People's war and Janashakti leaders were accorded a warm reception when they came for talks with the Government in Hyderabad. They were also given a safe passage into their hideouts in Nallamala forests. The media, both electronic and print, gave them wide coverage. All this hype gave the impression that the government was at fault, but not the Naxals.

The PW refused to say 'farewell to arms' and give up their line of armed struggle. The government acquiesced in this untenable posture and gave those concessions and publicity. PWG transformed itself into yet another incarnation called CPI (Maoist) to be an appendage of the MCC (Maoist Communist Centre) of Bihar and other adjoining states. It implies that all the splinter groups of Naxals in the country made a common cause to form a unified command and control.

These outfits intend to form a Maoist corridor across the country from AP to Nepal through Odisha, Chhattisgarh, Jharkhand, Bengal and Bihar. Now, is the Naxal corridor any different from that of Jinnah's partition plan of 1947 for a corridor to link eastern and western wings Pakistan?

❖❖❖

138. BUSH WIN

George W. Bush has retained the United States presidency for a second consecutive term, as his worthy Democratic challenger John Kerry magnanimously conceded defeat, even before the last vote is counted in the crucial state of Ohio.

Thus, Kerry saved the US and the rest of the world from the excruciating wait for the result for some more days, as was the case in 2000 elections.

The victory of Bush could be the vindication of his overbearing policies on Iraq. The American voters obviously concluded that their country is safe in the hands of Bush.

But, is it safe for the rest of the world? Only the coming months and years would reveal it. In the Indian sub-continent, Bush may, in all probability, pursue his pro-Pakistan policy more vigorously than ever before. In turn, this could be to the detriment of Indian interests.

❖❖❖

139. UMA'S OUSTER

Uma Bharti's unceremonious suspension from the BJP under the leadership of L.K. Advani raised many eyebrows. There can be no two opinions that she is one of the most outspoken leaders in the country.

That she is the only crowd puller in the BJP with the possible exception of Advani need not be overemphasized.

That she can activate and arouse the pent-up passions of masses into frenzy is unquestionable. That she is the architect of BJP's electoral victory in Madhya Pradesh in the last Assembly elections speaks volumes of her importance in the party. She is also among the few with an unblemished record in her political career.

The BJP hierarchy should weigh the pros and cons of the matter before initiating any precipitate action against her.

❖❖❖

140. NIGHT ARRESTS

The arrest of Sri Jayendra Saraswati, the Sankaracharya of the Kanchi Kamakoti Peetham, on Nov 11 by Tamil Nadu police, implicating him in a murder case is most unfortunate. It is intriguing that the arrest was done in the night. Earlier, Dravida Munnetra Kazhagam supremo M. Karunanidhi was also arrested in Chennai at midnight. It has become a custom for this government to go in for the arrest of VIPs only in the night. The respected pontiff under arrest has offered valuable suggestions on contentious issues including the Ram Mandir construction at Ayodhya. That a person of his eminence would have stooped to such criminal activities is beyond the comprehension of any right-thinking person. His arrest would certainly provide a major issue for the BJP and its followers to arraign the government at the Centre. It is hoped that the seer would come out unscathed from the imbroglio.

❖❖❖

141. SECULAR ETHOS OF HINDUISM

BJP president L.K. Advani in his address to the party's national executive meeting at Ranchi, discussed secularism on the basis of Hindu ethos.

Ethos is the spirit of a community, people or system. The Hindu ethos comprises the dual traits of accommodation and tolerance of other faiths. One can be an atheist and still be a Hindu without let or hindrance. This is not possible in other religions wherein non-believers and non-conformists are not tolerated.

Any religion, by definition, is based on the belief in a superhuman force and faith, devotion and worship of the same. The so-called Hinduism is not a religion at all as understood and followed. It is a way of life, followed by the people in this land of Bharata Varsha, since time immemorial. It is propagated and sustained by sages of yore like Veda Vyas, Adi Sankaracharya of Kaladi and Mandan Mishra of Varanasi.

The word 'Hindu' is a derivative of 'Sindhu' which means an ocean. No person could claim to be the founder of this religion. There is no authoritative or standard scriptures for Hinduism like Bible, Quran or Guru Granth Saheb for the people to emulate. Only Bhagwan Krishna codified and enunciated the salient postulates and principles of Hindu dharma through his divine poems constituting '*Bhagavad Gita*'. Even this one does not meet the norms of religious text.

The diversified nature of Hinduism and its infinite tolerance towards fellow beings is responsible for the survival of various religious systems in this ancient country.

In the final analysis, Mahatma Gandhi and Nehru were born Hindus and hence they were secular. Though Moulana Abul Kalam Azad was secular Muslim to the core, he was an Arab, born in Mecca. Even now there are quite a few Indian Muslims who profess to be secular like Rafiq Zakaria and M.J. Akbar.

❖❖❖

142. DIVINE RIGHT

Bharatiya Janata Party President L.K. Advani recently proclaimed that BJP is the chosen instrument of the Divine, to solve the country's problems. Perchance, he might have invoked the Hindu belief 'Na Vishnu Prithvipati' which implies that divinity resides in the king. In essence, it postulates that any person could be a king by virtue of divine commandment but not by popular mandate.

True, the high and the mighty did always think that they were in their exalted positions due to divine dispensation. The theory of 'Divine Right' was first propounded by the 16th century British King Henry VIII. This proposition came to nought in 17th century Britain, when Parliament forces led by Oliver Cromwell defeated the army of King Charles and publicly executed him outside Whitehall Palace.

Now, where does Advani fit in this background story of Divine right—a king or a hero? Obviously, he is neither. He only spoke out of frustration caused by his party's defeat in the recent parliamentary elections and subsequent Assembly elections. In effect, Advani did a disservice to the party he presides over, by his doctrine of infallibility and divine right of his party to govern this country.

❖❖❖

143. UNSUNG HERO

The Telugu 'Velugu' (light) P.V. Narasimha Rao has died unsung. His party, the Congress led by Sonia Gandhi ditched him in the later part of his life. He could have been easily accommodated as a senior statesman in the party working committee, in view of his varied experience in myriad fields. But, it was not to be.

Sonia Gandhi's discomfiture with Rao was so telling that she, as Congress president, did not even grace his funeral rites in Hyderabad, though she sent her representatives. In contrast, Prime Minister Manmohan Singh and a few of his colleagues attended Rao's last journey. P.V.'s intellectual prowess and analytical ability were so unparalleled that he was able to discern between the reality and rhetoric which punctuated the reigns of Jawaharlal Nehru and Indira Gandhi. These distinguishing characteristics led him to launch economic reforms under the aegis of his able Finance Minister

Manmohan Singh, thus deviating from the Nehru model of socialistic pattern of mixed economy, during his stewardship as prime minister in the nineties (1991-96). He was also responsible for containing the decade-long insurgency in Punjab. In fact, he brought a paradigm shift in India's economic and foreign policies. And he was not suitably rewarded for his commendable achievements in these fields during his life-time.

❖❖❖

144. PREZ NATIONALITY

This has reference to the news item 'Could Foreign-born Become US Prez'. Democratic Congressman Brad Sherman of California and John Canyers of Michigan together introduced a novel constitutional amendment in the Congress purporting to enlarge the presidential eligibility criteria. It seeks to allow any foreign-born person who has been a US citizen for 20 years or more to run for the US Presidency. It is a revolutionary measure with far-reaching results.

In the beginning, such a measure would allow persons of foreign origin like Arnold Schwarzenegger, the California Governor to aspire for a presidential nomination to contest for the high office. It may be perceived that California is the home for quite a significant cluster of Indian Americans. In course of time, any influential Indian American could seek nomination of either a Democratic or Republican Party, to be in the race for the White House.

Such a scenario may also be easily created in India. Following the footprints of American law-makers, Indian Parliamentarians may also initiate a similar legislation in the Lok Sabha to allow foreign born citizens to contest for the highest offices in the land including that of Prime Minister or President, provided they satisfy a time-bound Indian citizenship for more than 20 years. It removes all legal hurdles for such people.

❖❖❖

145. SINO-INDIAN TANGLE

The concept of SAARC (South Asian Association for Regional Cooperation) was implemented during Rajiv Gandhi's regime (1984-89), for the economic integration of the subcontinent. The report 'Will India and Bhutan let China into SAARC forum?' suggests that Pakistan and Bangladesh will make efforts at the forthcoming SAARC summit at Dhaka to bring in China into the ambit. Their move is to browbeat India's interests and provide a counter-weight to India in the region. Otherwise, what has China got to do with a regional grouping like the SAARC?

China has boundary disputes not only with India but with Bhutan and ASEAN nations as well. Their intentions are suspect due to their expansionist designs. Such hegemonic motives have led to their invasion of an unprepared India across the Himalayas in October 1962. Only Vietnam could fight the PLA (People Liberation Army) of China and thwart their southward expansion in the 1970s.

China has the least compunction in frustrating India's efforts to join the Shanghai Cooperation Organization (SCO), if only to minimize and eventually eliminate India's influence, if any, in the Central Asian republics which are also members of SCO along with China and Russia. It is also pertinent to take cognizance that, in addition to the US, China also is a supplier of weapons to Pakistan. All this should be the guide for India in the formulation of its relations with China.

❖❖❖

146. MAOIST THREAT AND INDIA'S ROLE

The recent developments in Nepal have not been considered in their right perspective. There is a Maoist insurgency threatening to engulf the country. The democratic government of Sher Bahadur Deoba failed to maintain law and order by containing the Maoist threat.

Democracy by itself is not sacrosanct, when it fails to protect the lives and properties of its citizens. King Gyanendra enforced emergency, dismissing the Deoba government and took over the reins of power.

India's response to these events in Nepal is unrealistic. India withdrew itself from the SAARC summit at Dhaka, if only to avoid rubbing shoulders with King Gyanendra. But, it has no qualms to talk to the die-hard leaders of Pakistan's military-guided democracy and Burma's military junta. The Indian army has a Nepalese regiment whose sentiments for the King have to be respected. Now, will India remain a passive spectator to Maoist takeover of Nepal, as it did when China invaded Tibet in the 1950s. The Maoist menace in India is disrupting peace in the states from Andhra Pradesh in the south to Bihar in the north, bordering Nepal. And so, the Maoist threat can be ignored at or own peril. It is in our own interest to supply sufficient arms and ammunition to Nepal to fight the Maoists. If it becomes absolutely necessary, our Army contingents have to be sent to Nepal to assist the King in his mission to crush the Maoist insurgents.

❖❖❖

147. AID TO NEPAL

This has reference to the news item 'India, UK Suspend Military Aid to Nepal'. The United States, India and Britain condemned King Gyanendra's declaration of emergency in Nepal together with abrogation of its democratic institutions. But China termed the event as an internal matter. While China and India border with Nepal on either side, the US and United Kingdom are far away from it and as such have no stakes in its affairs. The US and China may not take any punitive action against Nepal. But, UK and India have reacted sharply now. They have even suspended military supplies to Nepal, thus pressurizing it to restore democracy.

The UK has its own agonizing history of internecine conflicts between the monarchy and Parliament. Only in the 17th century, the King's absolute powers had been curtailed, as a sequel to a bloody war between Charles-I's Army and Parliament's 'Roundhead Army' under Oliver Cromwell, resulting in the King's defeat and execution. In course of time, Britain opted for constitutional monarchy, thus making the King only a figure-head without any worthwhile powers.

Now, in view of its history, would it be logical on its part to pressurize Gyanendra to restore democracy in Nepal?

In the final analysis, it would be in all fairness to Nepal, if Britain, not only restores its supply of military hardware to Nepal but also substantially increases it to enable the King to terminate Maoist insurgency. Restoration of democracy can wait till Maoists are eliminated. India should follow suit and vigorously pursue such a line of action towards Nepal, working in tandem with Britain.

❖❖❖

148. JUDICIARY WINS

The Supreme Court's recent order on the Jharkhand issue is historic, even though it encroached upon the political space, after the politicians themselves approached it. Its remarks of a fraud on the Constitution in the appointment of Shibu Soren as Chief Minister by Governor Syed Sibtey Raji and its directive to advance Assembly meeting to March 11 for a composite floor test constitute a moral and political setback to UPA Government.

But, its order came to naught when the pro-tem Speaker Pradip Balamuchu adjourned the Assembly that day without holding the trial of strength, thus placing him in confrontation with the apex court.

However, sensing the impending clash with the judiciary, the Union Cabinet gave marching orders to Soren which paved the way for a new setup under Arjun Munda of the BJP.

The truth is that the Jharkhand Governor acted the way he did to install a minority government in the state on the unimaginative bidding of the UPA chairperson Sonia Gandhi. Even so, the sycophants in the Congress tried to distance her away from the turmoil when the events became too hot to handle. But, this affair did incalculable harm to the UPA government headed by Manmohan Singh.

Even Sonia Gandhi who wields power without responsibility through remote control, would not escape public repulsion on this score, since Dr. Singh acts according to her fancies.

Now, the question is about the functioning of the executive, legislature and judiciary, within their respective domains as per the provisions enunciated by the Constitution. None of these entities are supreme by themselves, save only the Constitution. When there are large-scale violations of the constitutional provisions by the executive and legislature, judicial activism becomes absolute necessary to intervene so as to set things right as in the present case.

❖❖❖

149. BIASED PUNCH

Close on the heels of American Secretary-of-State Condoleezza Rice's visit to India and the bonhomie thereof, the decision of the Bush administration to impound the diplomatic and tourist visas of Narendra Modi, imparts a rude shock to Indian. It is a kind of continuing love-hate relationship between the United States and India.

However, it is quite another matter that the US quotes our NHRC report in this context, thus punching our eyes with our own finger.

The US decision hits the nail on the head for Modi. Even so, it is tantalizing and ludicrous. It has hurt the largest democracy in the world without any benefit of doubt, as Modi himself expressed so, in disgust. The Government has done well in lodging a protest with the US, rising above petty political parties interests. It also preferred a missive to the US to reconsider its decision.

India is capable of dealing with Modi. The editorial also commends this point. Now, there are large-scale human rights' violations among the minorities, including the Shia sect of Muslims, both in Pakistan and Bangladesh. Would the US snub these countries and their leaders, and in particular those of Pakistan? I hope, it will not, as Pakistan is its most favoured and natural non-NATO ally.

❖❖❖

150. F-16S TO PAK

Napoleon Bonaparte once called England as 'a nation of shop keepers'. True to the spirit, "The English" came to India for trade as foot-soldiers of British East India Company and subsequently became the rulers of the sub-continent. Now, their cousins across the

Atlantic Ocean, viz., the Americans seem to confirm the Napoleonic description of them.

The Bush administration's decision to supply F-16 jet fighters to Pakistan, held up for 15 long years, is patently a business transaction, over-ruling India's reservations in the matter. Pakistan can, at the most, buy over a dozen of these war planes.

But, India's projected requirement is much more a staggering quantity of 126x supersonic fighter aircraft, for which it was in touch with a few aviation majors in Europe and elsewhere, including Lockheed Martin of the United States.

And, the American decision is meant to allow its aviation giant Lockheed Martin to compete with the other aviation companies, for a share in India's massive shopping list which could easily amount to over $3 billion. In this background and as if to mollify the ruffled Indian sentiments, the US has offered to India F-16 fighters, as also its improved version F-18s catering to Indian specifications if required, along with visions of both joint production and technology transfer of the same.

The Bush Administrate fact has to find lucrative market for the America military-industrial complex which needs uninterrupted sale of its munitions to keep it going in full-steam. All this will lead to a conventional arms race between India and Pakistan to the benefit of the American Military merchants. The immediate fallout of their trade-related supply of military hardware to Pakistan would be to embolden its military-cum-civilian ruler Gen. Pervez Musharraf to harp on his pet core theme of Kashmir from a position of strength and browbeat India to extract quite a few concessions on the so-called issue during his forthcoming visit to India. This deals a body blow to the on-going peace moves between the two countries.

❖❖❖

151. END OF AN ERA

The passing away of Pope John Paul II, the high priest of Catholic community the world over, though grievous was inevitable. Some other worthy person would, of course, take his place. Nothing would stop. This is the way of the world.

The kingliest of kings (to use the phrase of Sarojini Naidu, the Nightingale of India), the high and the mighty, the rich and the poor, the famous and the ordinary, one and all must succumb to death one day or the other. Death is the leveller of all human beings without differentiation or discrimination. In Sanskrit, it is said *"Jatasya Maranam Dhruvam"*. It implies that death is certain for all those who take birth. Even Bhagwan Rama and Bhagwan Krishna who assumed human form for divine purposes in this mortal world had to meet the ultimate death, in one way or the other.

In this contest, I am reminded of the famous poem of H.W. Longfellow and I quote:

The glories of our blood and state
Are shadows, not substantial things
There is no armour against fate
Death lays his icy hand on kings
Sceptre and crown
Must tumble down
And in the dust be equal made
With the poor crooked scythe and spade
Only the actions of the just
Smell sweet and blossom in their dust.

❖❖❖

152. CHINA-PAK AXIS

This has reference to the news item 'China Won't Back India's Council Bid: Pakistan'. First, China and Pakistan act *in tandem* when India's national interests are the theme. Secondly, the China-Pakistan axis is very active to checkmate India's growth as a regional power in Asia-Pacific domain and as a power; to reckon with in international spectrum. China's efforts to enter SAARC, a strictly sub-continental grouping are a pointer in this regard. Viewed in this perspective, our External Affairs Ministry's interpretation of Chinese premier Wen Jiabao's remarks during his recent visit to India after his sojourn in Pakistan that China is supportive of India's bid to become a permanent member of UN Security Council is ill-conceived and unwarranted.

In this context, I recall our first Prime Minister Jawaharlal Nehru's remarks in one of his letters to the Chief Ministers of the day, before the Chinese invasion of India in Oct 1962. He opined that it is possible to live peacefully with the Soviet Union (now Russia), but it does not appear to be possible to do that with China and hence the essential conflict. It is hoped that our policy-makers in South Block mandarins keep this aspect in view, in their confabulations with China on the border question in the coming months.

❖❖❖

153. LALU IMBROGLIO

Railway Minister Lalu Prasad Yadav has become the Achilles heel for the UPA Government. Resigning on his own, when a court of law framed charges of corruption against him in the fodder scam would have been honourable for him and saved the Manmohan Singh Government from embarrassment. But he has taken umbrage under the legal postulate of presumption of innocence unless proved guilty, in the criminal justice system. Lalu controls 29 faithful votes in the Lok Sabha and this number is crucial for the survival of the UPA Government. The Prime Minister's rejection of BJP-led NDA's demand for the removal of the charge-sheeted Lalu is related to this fact. Of course, he has no mandate to dissolve his own government, thus enacting a political 'Harakiri'. However, it is time that the treasury benches and the Opposition worked out a consensus on the proposition that a charge-sheeted person should not be kept as a minister unless acquitted by the court.

❖❖❖

154. BOYCOTT

BJP-led NDA's decision to continue its boycott of Parliament till the end of the Budget session and its obduracy in rejecting the advice of Speaker Somnath Chatterjee to terminate its protest is unfortunate. The pertinent question is whether our Parliament is to be paralysed to perpetual disfunction, as the Opposition is invariably at loggerheads with the treasury benches?

The Westminster model of democracy adopted by the founders of our Constitution requires a modicum of rationality, maturity and morality on the pan of the legislators. But, it is obvious that Indian polity has progressively discarded all these unwritten criteria of our Constitution, without the least compunction.

Tainted Railway Minister Lalu Prasad Yadav's continuation in the Cabinet is a case in point. The catch phrase 'compulsions of coalition polities', conveniently coined by our honourable Prime Minister Manmohan Singh, to shield his sizeable corrupt ministers, does not stand to reason. NDA too has its own share of skeletons in its cupboard, while it was on the treasury benches, not long ago. With such unwholesome scenario, it can be easily apprehended that our present democratic system operated by unscrupulous politicians will lead us to Heisenberg's principle of uncertainty.

❖❖❖

155. BLAIR'S THIRD TERM

British Prime Minister Tony Blair first rode to power with a thumping majority in 1997, thus terminating the Conservative party's reign for a considerable under the period under the Iron-lady Margaret Thatcher and then John Major. He repeated his success story in 2001 elections. Now, he won a third term for himself and his Labour Party, though with a reduced majority in the elections held on May 5, a remarkable feat indeed. He is the only Labour leader after the Conservative Thatcher to win three elections in a row. Blair made his intention clear to go in for a third term. He is 52 and if he so desires could even stay for a fourth term, provided he leads his party to victory in the 2009 elections.

Blair could lead the Party by virtue of his imaginative internal policies, though he was hamstrung due to his unstinted support to US President George Bush's Iraq war which caused many a heartburn to the British public, as many British soldiers were killed during this unholy war. The Labour Party was understandably happy over its victory at the hustings but it had to reckon with its dwindling popularity over the Iraq question.

❖❖❖

156. G-4 SUMMIT

Necessity is the mother of invention. This axiom has been unwittingly confirmed by the Group of four nations, when they decided to collaborate with one another for their quest for permanent membership in the UN Security Council, with veto-wielding powers. These four—India, Japan, Germany and Brazil—belong to different cultures, religions and regions. Still, they have reinvented themselves to forge together to achieve their rightful place in the comity of nations. They have recently circulated a draft resolution to 80 member-states of the UN. Thanks to their adroitness, it is a well-timed diplomatic master-stroke, as there are two more draft resolutions before the UN General Assembly, for eventual expansion of the 5-permanent member Security Council, to transform it to be more representative.

The odds are more or less against the success of this concerted effort of G-4. Each of the four countries has to contend with at least one regional force, acting in the opposite direction. These rivals are China-Pakistan axis for India, China for Japan, Italy for Germany and Argentina and Chile for Brazil. The United States is non-committal, though it supports its faithful ally Japan. Further, troubles may crop up, as G-4 chooses two yet unidentified African countries aspiring to permanent membership–Egypt and Nigeria. And the state kept out from such a 'Group of six' may work against the ambitious project. Even so, if they could muster support of two-thirds or 128 members of 191-strong UN, then they would achieve their objective. The uncertainty of G-4 initiative is effectively reflected in the editorial, though it is made out that G-4 could be a force to reckon with, in world councils.

❖❖❖

157. BIHAR POLLS

Before dissolving the nascent Bihar Assembly and thus opting for fresh elections in nine months, Prime Minister Manmohan Singh could have easily assessed the cost-effectiveness and feasibility of such a retrograde step. Can the national exchequer afford the enormous expenditure involved in the unwarranted exercise? His justification of the disputable decision on the basis of 'horse-trading of the worst kind' is a lame excuse. The dictionary meaning of 'horse-trading' is 'hard-bargaining'. So, what is wrong with it? It is inherent in the formation of coalition governments. Money transactions are not necessarily its criteria.

The UPA government itself was the result of hard-bargaining for the loaves and fishes to be distributed among the partners. It is certainly not a group of saints to assume a high moral ground. So, it is clear that horse-trading is made a convenient ploy by the ruling coterie at the Centre to forestall the formation of NDA government in Bihar under Nitish Kumar. This is only to satisfy the ego of Railway Minister Lalu Prasad Yadav who has a very few peers in comedian polemics of blackmail, like Raj Narain of yesteryears.

❖❖❖

158. SECULARISM

This has reference to the article 'The Shame of Secularism' by Balbir K. Punz. The so-called secularism of Congress led UPA government had been a negation without doubt, when they denied Indian citizenship to renowned Bangladeshi writer Taslima Nasreen who was hounded out by Islamic clergy from her home country for her alleged apostasy, in authoring the novel 'Lazza'. However, it being the creed of Congress and its fellow travellers to appease Muslim clergy and bash Hindus and their clergy, this act of Lazza (shame) is no big surprise. Shah Bano case during Rajiv Gandhi's reign is glaring example of the same. In fact, the secular character of the Congress regime became void, when all its three leaders – Sardar Patel, Pandit Nehru and Mahatma Gandhi – bartered the June 3 partition plan of Lord Louis Mountbatten, for achieving independence, thus unwillingly endorsing Mohammed Ali Jinnah's pernicious two-nation theory and dividing India on religious lines. The writer's fears of formation of Bang-e-Islam with the inclusion of all North-eastern states including Bengal and north Bihar are farfetched. In comparison to India's flourishing economy and mighty armed forces, Bangla could be no match at all. It can never achieve such a scenario of partitioning India's north-eastern provinces, even in its dreams. At the most, it can engage in infiltration of trained armed-insurgents into these regions to create havoc and terror, following the footsteps of Islamic Pakistan. But, it is the duty of the Centre to defend and protect our eastern borders against any unfriendly incursions.

❖❖❖

159. PATHAN SACRIFICES

This refers to Kuldip Nayar's article 'Democracy is a Question Mark' He says "it may be that Pakistan has not gone through the Independence struggle as India has or Muslim League has not suffered or made sacrifices the way the then Congress Party did". The first-half of hist assertion is only partly true while the second-half about the Muslim League is true. Of the four Pakistan provinces, NWFP (North West Frontier Province, now, 'Khyber Phaktunkhwa') took pro-active part in Mahatma Gandhi's non-violent non-cooperation movements, under the charismatic leadership of Frontier Gandhi Khan Abdul Gaffar Khan who raised disciplined Pathan soldiers of non-violence, – 'Khudai Khidmatgars (servants of God)'. But the Congress, while accepting the then Viceroy Lord Louis Mountbatten's June 3, 1947 partition plan, did not take into consideration the sacrifices of its trusted lieutenants 'the Khan Brothers' Gaffar Khan and Dr. Khan Sahib — and left them and their Pathan followers to their fate. The Congress did not even participate in the referendum conducted in NWFP to ascertain Pathans preference, with the result that it went with Pakistan with a wafer-thin majority. In dismay, the Frontier Gandhi admonished Mahatma Gandhi saying, "you have thrown us to the wolves" (Muslim Leaguers). True to his words, he had to spend 20 years in Pakistan jails, due to his Congress connection and wanton indiscretion.

Yes, as Nayar opined, Pakistanis (except perhaps Pathans) have reconciled to military rule. They have no tradition of upholding their birth-right of freedom, as Indians did under the stewardship of Gandhi. Nayar's prediction that Pakistan may opt for a Turkey-like structure someday may be an optimistic thinking. If it happens, it would be a blessing for Pakistanis, as Turkey is an ultra-modern liberal democracy, adopted to its own circumstances, culture and ethics.

❖❖❖

160. ADVANI EMERGES STRONGER

During his tour of Pakistan, L.K. Advani took care to do justice to both his religion and the hosts. If he made his mythological marches into Sri Rama's son Lav's temple in Lahore Fort and Katas Raj temple complex near Rawalpindi, then he also made a historical visit to Mohammed Ali Jinnah's mausoleum in Karachi. At the Karachi monument, he described Jinnah as a great man who created history. He quoted Jinnah's Aug 11, 1947 address to the Constituent Assembly, wherein he said, "Hindus will cease to be Hindus and Muslims will cease to be Muslims, not in the religious sense, because that is the personal faith of each individual but in the political sense will be citizens of the state". By these words, Jinnah could not be termed as 'secular', as he was the originator of the two-nation theory, separating Hindus and Muslims. It was only his selfish motive to keep the minorities (Hindus) in Pakistan out of his love for their money that made him speak the way he did. But, as expressed by Advani, he was really great as he was the architect-founder of the Islamic-theocratic state of Pakistan, though moth-eaten, in his own words. While he gave a homeland to Muslims, Sardar Patel and Pandit Nehru together could not achieve 'a Hindu India' but only a secular Indian state. In the same vein, it can be said that Advani would not become 'secular' overnight by praising Jinnah.

Being an astute politician, he must have weighed the repercussions of his words, spoken in a neighbouring country. He took a calculated risk and gave a shock-therapy to BJP, dormant since 2004 Parliament election reverses. His gamble paid off and he withdrew his resignation as party president (submitted under fire-works from Sangh Parivar), when the BJP Parliamentary Board meeting of Jun 9 gave weightage to his Pakistan sojourn. By all means, Advani stood out from the rest and emerged stronger.

❖❖❖

161. CAGED TIGER

Nawab Mansur Ali Khan Pataudi is an honourable man. Animal rights activists had him arrested for alleged involvement in the killing of a black buck and two hares, belonging to endangered species. He was confined to a solitary cell without even electricity for a couple of days for police interrogation. When there was light, he was reading Arnold Toynbee's book "A Study of History". This, in itself, distinguishes him from a commoner. But, the pertinent question is whether it is absolutely essential to subject such a person of nobility to the indignities he suffered on flimsy charges, trumped up by the so-called animal lovers? He could have been questioned in his own mansion. This unsavoury episode suggests that man is born in tandem with jealousy and animal rights activists are no different. They should remember that human life itself is endangered due to unacceptable level of greenhouse gas emissions and indiscriminate disposal of Nuclear-waste. Let them first do something about it before resorting to pretend as saviours of animal life.

In this context, I recall an interesting incident when India was still a British subject. Pandit Jawaharlal Nehru was on a tour of troubled Bihar. The British government provided him police escort for his safety. Incensed by this act, Nehru commented that he was paraded like a criminal in Bihar. And the government kept its cool. Such was the indulgence of an alien government. My only regret is that, in free India, even an iota of indulgence is not allowed to celebrities like Tiger Pataudi.

❖❖❖

162. GANDHI *VS.* JINNAH

I refer to the editorial "Now, Let's Talk Gandhi". But, Mahatma Gandhi cannot be talked about in isolation. Gandhi and Jinnah are inter-linked by history. In view of the ongoing row over Jinnah's secularism raised by L.K. Advani, it would be pertinent to study Gandhi and Jinnah in contrast.

Gandhi was an apostle of non-violence and peace. But Jinnah believed in organised violence, as amplified by his 'Direct Action' of Aug 16, 1946, resulting in thousands of innocent deaths. While Gandhi worked, lived and died for Hindu-Muslim unity, viewing the two communities as his two eyes, though hindered by 'divide and rule' policy of English rulers, Jinnah postuated that Hindus and Muslims are two nations and worked whole-time to divide them.

The British Government under Ramsey Macdonald aided his theory by imposing 'Communal Award' in 1932. While Gandhi, by his non-violent non-cooperation movements, achieved independence of the whole Indian sub-continent from foreign yoke in 1947, Jinnah achieved partition of India, with the help of British rulers. While Gandhi was in agony that his life's mission was in a shambles, Jinnah was in ecstasy that he could establish a nation and homeland for Muslims.

Now, the question is why did Jinnah, being a nationalist in 1920s, transform into a communalist in later years? With the advent of Gandhi from South Africa on Indian political horizon and his meteoric rise in Congress as the mass-leader, Jinnah's aspirations to become a leader in his own right in Congress became degenerated. He said, "I have no place in Gandhi's Congress", before the start of Gandhi's non-cooperation movement in 1921. He drifted away from Congress, to become a rank communalist, leading the Muslim league. As a person, Jinnah was non-religious. He even married a Parsi. Gandhi was secular to the core, exemplified by his political life. And whatever RSS thinks of Gandhi and Jinnah, they cannot erase historical truths, as facts are facts.

❖❖❖

163. KASHMIR POLICY

This refers to Sumeer Kaul's article 'Need for a Coherent Policy'. I appreciate the writer's use of apt adjective phrases—'CEO of Two-nation Theory' and 'High Priest of Partiton' for late Mohammed Ali Jinnah and PR Commando and 'accomplished Janus' (ancient Italian two-faced God) for Gen. Pervez Musharraf.

Yes, Jinnah could achieve his dreamland of Pakistan in collusion with erstwhile British rulers, coupled with the weak-kneed appeasement policy of the then Congress. Now, Gen. Musharraf seems to be right on the way to annex part of Kashmir, the cherished objective of Jinnah who invaded this state in October 1947.

The Congress-led UPA Government is following the policy of the BJP-led NDA government in treating the General and his Kashmiri cohorts as if their words and deeds inimical to Indian interests, are gospel truths translated into actions, contributing to peace in the sub-continent.

It seems the UPA government is in a quagmire. It only acts admitting security lapses when the Jehadi-terrorists strike, as is evidenced in the Ayodhya imbroglio of July 5.

In Kashmir, such incidents are the order of the day. In a sort of ethnic-cleansing for the past decade, the Pandits were driven away from their hearths and homes in the Kashmir valley, by the Pak-trained militants and the government was a mute spectator. Secessionists were treated generously. But, the relevant question is why the government is fighting shy of creating a Kashmir-like situation in Sindh or Baluchistan? It would be a tit-for-tat shock-therapy for Pakistan. They would then only realise their folly of insurgency in Kashmir and come to terms with India.

❖❖❖

164. WAH TAJ!

Allahabad High Court known for its independent judicial decisions is sometimes controversial. This aspect was evidenced by Justice Jagmohan Lal Sinha's verdict in 1975, unseating the then reigning Prime Minister, Mrs. Indira Gandhi, attracting the Amercian Press interpretation that it was like awarding capital punishment for wrong parking. However, it became the fore-runner for subsequent cataclysmic political events.

Again, a few years ago, this court conferred legal status on young couple living together without marriage, which led to convulsions in Uttar Pradesh. Now again, acting on a petition by Irfan Bedar, the court gave direction to the UP Sunni Central Waqf Board which declared that Taj Mahal is a Waqf property! The attraction here is ₹ 15 crore annual income of the monument.

Taj Mahal, one of the seven wonders of the world, was built as a symbol of love and peace during the reign of Mogul emperor Shah Jehan (Khurram), in memory of his beloved wife Mumtaj Mahal (Arzumand Bano).

He followed the principle of equivalence of all religions before law, enunciated by his peers Jalaluddin Mohammed Akbar and Jehangir (Salim), his grandfather and father, respectively.

As such, it stands as a secular symbol and belongs to the whole of India and certainly not to a particular community. It is now under the administration of Archaeological Survey of India.

The present secular UPA Government should stand firm on this delicate issue and not abdicate its responsibility to administer and control this tourist paradise in the name of appeasing the minorities.

❖❖❖

165. PM'S TRIP ABROAD

Prime Minister Manmohan Singh's unqualified romance with the British system of governance at Oxford university, during his visit to the UK was puzzling. Even Americans, their cousins across the Atlantic who battled with the British for their independence in the 18th century would not have opined likewise. Good alien rule is no substitute for home rule.

The British came to India for business, saw the untapped resources and conquered the country, as did Napoleon in Europe, in 16th century. They laid communication network including Railways only to perpetuate and tighten their stronghold on India. Urged on by Thomas Macaulay, they brought English language to educate and create a class of local *babus*, for easier communication. They built huge mansions in Delhi like Viceregal Lodge (the present Rashtrapati Bhavan) to house their viceroys in royal comfort and North and South Blocks to house their administrative machinery and men. All this was done with our money. They certainly did not come to India to provide us good government. Nobody can contend that India would have remained in stagnation of medieval centuries, had the British not stepped into the country. China was not under the British rule but still it could steal a march over others, compatible with modern times. In this context, the NDA move to censure the Prime Minister in Parliament for his Oxford university address is quite apt.

❖❖❖

166. NUKE PACT

The Washington agreement of July 16 between Prime Minister Manmohan Singh and President George W. Bush is inimical to Indian interests on nuclear programmes, though not a virtual sell-out. The US proclaimed its intention for full civil nuclear energy cooperation with India, a responsible state with advanced nuclear technology. In return, India leapt a quantum jump backwards in conceding the US demand to place its civilian nuclear plants under International Atomic Energy Agency safeguards. As stone-walling between civil and military facilities in the nuclear field is impossible in India, IAEA's monitoring of non-military nuclear energy facilities would, not only jeopardize our Fast Breeder Reactor research projects but also hamper our nuclear weapons programme.

Again, India's reiteration of its commitment of moratorium on nuclear tests in the bilateral agreement without securing any concession is unnecessary and against our national interests. India could have insisted on US to declare a corresponding time-bound moratorium on its nuclear weapons projects. Well! It could not even wrest US support for its quest for UN Council membership. If matters retard this way, then there is likelihood of India becoming a responsible satrap of the US like Britain soon.

❖❖❖

167. TACTICAL ERROR

In his speech in the Rajya Sabha on August 4, Prime Minister Manmohan Singh spoke of the wisdom of opening up of our civilian nuclear energy sector to international inspection regime, in return for the US supplies of nuke fuel and technology. He said it was "a risk worth taking" as we would, eventually, be put on a higher growth path. But, it is doubtful whether the non-nuclear proliferation laws would be amended in India's favour by the US Congress, as averred by President George W. Bush.

Nuclear power plants produce 'reactor-grade' plutonium (Pu) which is also used, in addition to weapons-grade Pu, to build nuclear warheads.

The requirement of reactor-grade Pu is 8.0 kg and that of weapons-grade Pu is only 5.0 kg, for a warhead manufacture. Hence, our unilateral commitment on civil nuclear projects would adversely affect our nuclear weapons programme. It is a case of grave tactical and technical error.

❖❖❖

168. MANOHAR CASE

Very recently, there were two rare court cases involving capital punishment. One is that of Y. Manohar who committed a cold-blooded murder of his class-fellow R. Srilakshmi in Vijayawada. As it is only the sessions court which awarded the death sentence to the accused, he may prefer an appeal to the higher court. The other case is that of Mohammed Afzal, an accomplice of the slain terrorists who carried out the Dec 13, 2001 gruesome attack on Parliament, resulting in the death of nine security personnel.

The Supreme Court confirmed the death penalty awarded to him by lower courts. These are befitting and rarest of the rare cases where in capital punishment will do justice to the aggrieved.

Now, those who cannot induct life have no rights to extinguish life whatever be their grievance. Such persons minds are filled with darkness over the ages and they commit sins with impunity. Though death penalty may not altogether curb criminal activities, it may at least, act as a deterrent in not allowing them to get scot-free, after perpetrating merciless murder and mayhem.

Its abrogation implies that the country is pledging these criminal elements that their life will not be endangered, even if they kill or rape people with recklessness. Such a perspective would be disastrous for the country.

❖❖❖

169. YSR LACKS WILL

When there is a will, there is a way. Yes. The YSR government lacks the will to govern firmly without wavering. It seem that it is a prisoner of indecision. Had it not been so, the Maoist menace would have been contained long ago. The government waited until the inhuman shooting down of Matkal MLA C. Narsi Reddy (76) and his followers by Maoist henchmen before imposing a ban on the Maoists and their adjuncts.

In the light of this perspective, Prime Minister Manmohan Singh's assertion that "extremism of any form cannot be tolerated in a civilized democratic society", seems incompatible with the ground realities. It is the Congress government that has tolerated all sorts of extremism, resulting in its growth to unmanageable proportions. A case in point is the unimaginative handling of the Maoist problem in our state. Conferring them equal status across the negotiating table, even as they refused to lay down their arms, was indeed a retrograde measure. The Maoists took the government for a ride and strengthened themselves with ammunition, arms and fresh recruits, during the uneasy peace period. Be that as it may, the government should, at least now, tackle the daunting situation by providing necessary and sufficient teeth to the police to eliminate the Maoists once and for all in Andhra Pradesh and other infected states.

❖❖❖

170. MOB VIOLENCE

In civil societies, which have experienced traumatic mob violence on a massive scale, apologies by the perpetrators are not considered a substitute for impartial judicial verdicts.

Apologies are generally intended as "a cover-up" for criminal acts of mayhem and vandalism. Viewed in this perspective, Prime Minister Manmohan Singh's recent but belated apology to the Sikh community and the nation, for the anti-Sikh riots, in the wake of the then Prime Minister Indira Gandhi's assassination on October 31, 1984, sounds hollow.

Singh has, however, opened a Pandora's box. If apologies are to be valued as authentic and genuine, then somebody has to apologize for the killing of Indira Gandhi, for the massacre of innocent Hindus during the militancy in Punjab and for Sant Bhindranwale's criminal acts by converting the Golden temple into a veritable fortress. And as nobody would be interested in this scheme of apologies, we should try to emulate South Africa's 'Truth and Reconciliation' process, wherein the perpetrators confess their crimes without fear of being victimized.

❖❖❖

171. ADVANI DAYS

Bharatiya Janata Party president L.K. Advani seems to be swirling in the vortex of an unfavourable time-wrap. First, his labelling Mohd. All Jinnah as secular was quixotic in nature; the resultant acrimonious wrangling in the Sangh Parivar was his own making. It could safely be attributed to his old-age oddity. However, this unwholesome chapter came to a close with nobody claiming victory.

Secondly, close on its heels, came the unavoidable rustication of Madan Lai Khurana, a long-standing party-faithful. In the episode, the boot is on the other leg, as Khurana himself invited his banishment, with his intemperate language against Advani. Even so, elder statesman Atal Behari Vajpayee chose to overtly support Khurana. In the same vein, he declared that he had no differences with his friend Advani. The ambiguity of Vajpayee made matters fluid for Advani. Ultimately, Advani, the modern Bhishma of the party was forced to revoke the expulsion of Khurana, thanks to the efforts of Vajpayee and RSS.

All is well that ends well. But, in the process, Advani had to coolly pocket the insults hurled at him by the irrepressible Khurana. Be it as it may, BJP being the only party unhindered by dynastic culture needs to reorganize itself as a unified party, by resolving its petty squabbles. Advani should take the initiative to manage and organize the party shrewdly, accommodating varied opinions and people like Khurana, if only he wants to overcome the challenges ahead in the party and the country as well, in the long run.

❖❖❖

172. DEATH FOR POST-75 PENSIONER?

Apropos the news report 'Long Life for Pensioners: A Curse or Boon', I would say it is really a grave news for the aging, retired government employees, propagating shock waves in them. Finance

Minister P. Chidambaram's purported statement on this account is ill-advised. It seems the government is against long life for its retired men, in fixing 75 years as Break Even Point (BEP) for them. If the prop by which they live is taken back during their twilight years, then on what support they are expected to fall back, to eke out a bare existence? Why this unwholesome disaffection towards septuagenarians?

At that ripe age, in addition to their food and clothing, they require medicines as well to keep them going, as most of them would be afflicted with some disease or other. Their pension would only, meet these expenses, as most of them are wholly dependent on it. Actually, pension is a social security measure providing succour to the old, inclusive of those obligations, since any system of governance is expected to look after the well-being of the aged and infirm. In fact, it should reward and not punish them for living so long to a ripe age. In Delhi itself, there is a practice of honouring the grand-old men, past hundred years or more. Taking a leaf out of this practice, the government should facilitate their living by providing more monetary incentives and follow the Sanskrit dictum *Satayuh Purushasya, Satamanam Bhavati.*

❖❖❖

173. QUOTING SCRIPTURES

TRS helmsman K. Chandrasekhar Rao can cite scriptures for his purpose. And so he cites Kavi Sarvabhowma (poet emperor) Srinatha to suit his speeches. If Srinatha spoke derisively of Palnadu's hard food, then he also spoke of Godavari districts' refined food in glowing terms. So, if at all, Palnadu Telugus might have migrated to Godavari districts and certainly not to Telangana districtsfor colonisation, as theorised by KCR taking umbrage under Srinatha's beautiful poetry. Actually, it was Vemulawada Bheema Kavi of Karimnagar district who migrated to Daksharamam in East Godavari district, being a devotee of the presiding deity 'Bheemeswara' of that town.

Again, KCR conveniently overlooks the fact that Andhra and Telugu are synonymous words for the language spoken in all the 23 districts of the state. Telangana is a variant of Telugu, appended to Telugu speaking region of erstwhile Nizam state. The movement of people from one region to another seeking greener pastures is a continuous natural process, occurring for varied reasons. And, it cannot be construed as colonisation. In spite of these home truths, let Telangana state be formed without further delay, as it has progressively become an Achilles heel for coastal and Rayalaseema areas.

❖❖❖

174. UNCIVILISED LANGUAGE

K. Chandrasekhar Rao, the big gun of TRS, is firing salvoes in an uncivilised manner against every person. His lieutenant A. Narendra is firing equally worse salvoes in a ferocious language. Though both are Congress-run UPA Government ministers, they have no compunction in deriding Congressmen with choicest invectives. And, the 'spineless wonder' Congress High Command meekly succumbs to KCR's blackmail tactics and advises the already silent Chief Minister YSR to maintain restraint.

The spicy language of KCR and his associate makes old-timers like me to remember the popular Hindi cinema 'Bluff Master' of yesteryears wherein Shammi Kapoor dons the title role.

I may, therefore, say KCR and his tribe may flourish without any impediment.

❖❖❖

175. KCR THEORY DOESN'T HOLD WATER

TRS President K. Chandrasekhar Rao is quoting classics selectively to suit his argument that people from Coastal Andhra districts came and colonized Telangana. If poet Srinatha spoke derisively about Palnadu region's hard food, as Mr. Rao is pointing out, then he also praised the refined food of Godavari districts. Therefore, it is possible that people from Palnadu region might have migrated to Godavari districts but not to Telangana as Mr. Rao theorised. In fact, it was Vemulawada Bheema Kavi who originally belonged to Karimnagar district, migrated to Daksharamam in East Godavari district, being a devotee of Bheemeswara, the presiding deity of the place. The movement of people from one region to another in search of better opportunities is a natural process that can't be called colonization. In spite of all this, if Telangana State is to be formed, let it be done without any further delay. It has progressively become an Achilles heel for coastal and Rayalaseema areas.

❖❖❖

176. TRS GUNS BOOM

Kalwakurthy Chandrasekhar Rao, the big gun of TRS is firing salvos of abusive language at random against all and sundry. His lieutenant A. Narendra is also using ferocious language helter-skelter from his AK-47 vocal rifle. Though both are cabinet ministers in the Congress-led UPA government, they have no compunction in deriding Congressmen with choicest invectives.

And, the boneless wonder called Congress high command meekly succumbs to KCR's blackmail tactics and vituperative language and advises the already silent Chief Minister Y.S. Rajasekhara Reddy to maintain restraint. In statistics, we learn about 'nuisance parameters'. It is hoped that KCR and his fellow-travellers do not wish to be listed under this category.

Even so, the spicy language of KCR and his associate reminds one of the popular Hindi film *Bluff Master* of yesteryears, wherein Shammi Kapoor dons the title role. I may, therefore, say KCR and his tribe may flourish without impediment.

However, now that they have been unequivocally discredited by the voters of Telangana, they should be more circumspect in hurling insinuations and invectives against their political adversaries. Discretion is better than valour.

❖❖❖

177. MINORITY INDIA

Napaleon Bonaparte had professed that "the English are a nation of shop-keepers". Following the footsteps of this postulate, we may say "India is a nation of minorities". Yes. My reference is to S. Gurumurthy's article 'A Country Full of Minorities'. This axiom based on Supreme Court's recent judgment rejecting Jain community's plea for minority status is thought-provoking. It is a matter of concern that we have not overcome the minorities reservations syndrome for over 50 years after our Constitution was adopted.

Various caste groups and communities crave for minority status to avail of privileges including reservations in educational institutions and government services at the entry level and for promotions thereafter. Such partisan rights are generously provided by successive governments both at the Centre and in the States, as a mode of vote-catching technique. In this context, the apex court's observation that an ever-increasing number of minority groups would sow the seeds of multi-nationalism, threatening the integrity of the country is appropriate. The court also cautioned the Minority Commission against allowing proliferation of the groups so that over a period, they are done away with altogether. These words of wisdom of Supreme Court must be needed by the government worth its salt, to discourage the craze of various communities for minority status, so that India may live without further vivisection.

❖❖❖

178. TRS CHIEF'S STATEMENTS

Union Cabinet Minister K. Chandrasekhar Rao and his colleague A. Narendra are firing salvos against all and sundry. Though both are Union Ministers in the UPA Government, they have no compunction and hesitation to issue derisive statements on the Congress party leaders. It seems the Congress high command has succumbed to Rao's tactics and his pungent language. Obviously, it has advised Chief Minister Y.S. Rajasekhara Reddy to maintain silence. The language of Rao and Narendra reminds old-timers like me of the hilarious Hindi cinema "Bluff Master" of yesteryears wherein Shammi Kapur dons the title role.

TRS leaders are doing the same now. Despite their big claims, they received a shock from the voters of Telangana in the recent municipal elections. They should better avoid confrontation at least now.

❖❖❖

179. INDIA STILL CAN MAKE AMENDS

The series of editorials culminating in India's interest first make a virtue of India's second fiddling to the United States in voting against Iran at IAEA governing board's meeting in Vienna on Sep 24 and turn the heat on Communists as villains for their criticism of the government. But, not only the Leftists but even the intelligentsia find it hard to stomach the government's partisan approach to the issue.

Though India was weak both economically and militarily, Jawaharlal Nehru, by shear force of his personality, was able to mobilize the world opinion against Britain of Anthony Eden and France, compelling them to vacate their invasion of Egypt for the control in 1956. Unfortunately now, though India is now strong enough to meet any challenge, we have a prime minister who is being operated by remote control and capsizes under pressure.

Being the sole super power, the US can impose its will on any country. Even Pakistan, a front-line state of US was forced to join American war on terror, ditching its own creation Taliban, under threat of 'carpet bombing'. And no doubt, India did succumb to American pressure, as was evidenced by Congressional hearings on Indo-US civil nuclear deal of July 18 (still in the form of a promise by US), wherein unjustified concern was orchestrated on Indo-Iranian relationship. Otherwise, it was inconceivable that India, a declared Nuclear weapons' state and a non-signatory to NFT could join with US and EU-3 (UK, France and Germany) in a proliferation indictment of Iran, a signatory to NPT in 1974 itself.

Perhaps, India does not favour another nuclear power like Iran in its vicinity in addition to Pakistan. But, in spite of India's volte-face, Iran was magnanimous enough to say that all agreements with India would be honoured, including $21 billion deal to supply 5 million LNG, as it appreciates that India stood by it in trying times.

In the whole episode, India emerged squarely mauled. However, it can make amends in the next IAEA meet in November, by not supporting US or EU move to take the Iranian problem to UN Security Council.

❖❖❖

180. UPA MUST LEAD

The Supreme Court's interim judgment declaring the dissolution of Bihar assembly on May 23 as 'unconstitutional' has dealt a body-blow to the blatant misuse of power by the executive. A consequent corollary of natural justice would have been the restoration of the defunct Assembly. It would have saved enormous expenditure in holding fresh elections in Bihar from Oct. 18, within a matter of seven months. But, it is strange that the court stopped short of ordering the inevitable resultant of its verdict. It is willing to strike but reluctant to wound?

However, the apex court by its historic order has notified that it would monitor executive actions and would be alert against any abuse of power by the government.

Now, in this murky episode, the Governor, the Prime Minister and the President are all on the wrong side of "Lakshman Rekha" of propriety and so each is accountable for his action. They should make amends for the unseemly haste in dissolving the House. But surprisingly, the Governor is asked to continue till a full-scale judgment of the apex court is delivered. The Prime Minister has accepted his moral responsibility and the President is keeping a studied silence, having allowed himself to be a rubber stamp by signing the government's missive while in Moscow. And so, it is better if the UPA itself takes the initiative in restructuring the government under an independent or undisputed leader.

❖❖❖

181. TREMORS ON LOC

The earthquake measuring 7.6 on the Richter scale on Oct. 8 caused death and destruction on either side of the Line of Control in Kashmir. The magnitude of the tremor was devastating in the Pak-occupied Kashmir. Each tragedy has its own lessons, if perceived in the right perspective. Both India and Pakistan have large populace on the southern flank of the Himalayan ranges.

It is here that the Indian sub-continent's tectonic plate is slowly thrusting against the main Asian continent, which results in killer quakes like the present one.

Such a seismic catastrophe should be instrumental in pushing the two nations closer than ever before.

But, this has not happened, as Pakistan rejected the Indian offer of joint operations to rescue the quake-hit and provide them succor, though they have received a material consignment from us.

However, it is gratifying to note that, our Army did a commendable job in helping the suffering Kashmiri people, thus striking a concordant note with them.

❖❖❖

182. CHANGE OF GUARD

I endorse the editorial 'In J&K, Freeze' Yes. Any change of guard in favour of Congress would be counterproductive. The Congress may have its own obligations to strengthen the party in J&K, particularly because it is in doldrums in all states but for a few exceptions like Andhra Pradesh. But it should take a long-term view to keep the present set-up lasting its term, as it is doing well on almost all fronts, unlike other Congress-ruled states.

Over the three years in power, Mufti Mohammed Sayed has emerged as the messiah of Kashmiris. He has conducted himself with dignity and integrity. He erased the impression among Kashmiris that the Chief Minister is an agent of Delhi. There is a sea change in the attitude of the people.

Their agenda is now provision of electricity, roads, schools and the like, as against secession or Azadi earlier, though it would be premature to assume that separatism has faded away altogether.

In the circumstances, political maturity and wisdom on the part of the Congress entails it to allow the Mufti to continue his commendable work for the remaining three years, even if it jeopardizes Congress prospects. The calculus of national interests should overweigh other considerations.

❖❖❖

183. MESSIAH OF KASHMIRIS

Over three years in power, Mufti Mohammed Sayed has emerged as the messiah of Kashmiris. He has conducted himself with dignity and integrity. He erased the impression among Kashmiris that J&K Chief Minister is a quisling. There is a sea change in the attitude of the people. Now, their agenda is provision of electricity, roads, schools, employment and the like as against secession or azadi earlier, though it would be premature to assume that separatism has faded away altogether. In the circumstances, political maturity and wisdom on the part of the Congress should have entailed it to allow the Mufti to continue his commendable work for the remaining three years, even if it jeopardises Congress prospects. But it was not to be.

All said and done, the calculus of Congress party interests overweighed national interests. It has played the role of 'Sakuni' of Mahabharat, preferred its candidate Ghulam Nabi Azad over the redoubtable Mufti. Though Azad is very efficient and shrewd, it remains to be seen how he deals with the myriad problems in Kashmir including the pernicious cross-border terrorism as he has been greeted with bomb blasts even before he took over as Chief Minister.

❖❖❖

184. PRIVATE ACTS IN PUBLIC PLACES

The pounding of love-lorn youth by Meerut women police personnel in the so-called 'Operation Majnu' unfolds their Talibanised mindset. The *raisen d'etre* of the operation is the indecent behaviour of teenage couples in public places. Surely, there are better methods available to the police women, for dealing with public display of acts of privacy by the youth, than thrashing them up.

Such couples could have been warned or put under arrest. Instead, the cops saw to it that their misplaced bravery and the resultant humiliation of the youth took place in the full glare of TV cameras. This reprehensible episode is another murky chapter in the annals of the not-so-encouraging police behavioural history.

The prime cause of such untoward incidents is the skewed perspective of moral values held by our society. But, this should not lead to police high-handedness in blatant disregard of fundamental rights of individuals. Attempts must be made to curb such incendiary tendencies of aboriginal nature during the training of police personnel. That being so, it seems 'Cupid', the God of love, should be more discreet in shooting his arrows on innocent youth of either sex, lest they be taken to task by the police.

❖❖❖

185. MORE GENERAL BOGIES NEEDED

The number of general compartments in express and super-fast trains is not enough to meet the requirements of the travelling public. At present, only two bogies nearer to the engine and two bogies at the tail-end of the train are being provided. These bogies are overcrowded, leaving little or no space even for standing. In particular, the elderly persons, women and children are facing the brunt of heavy rush in these bogies even for a short distance journey. During peak hours, the rush is worse and even able-bodied face difficulties. I request the railway authorities to increase the number of general bogies.

❖❖❖

186. PORTRAITS IN 'RED'

This is with reference to the news item "150 Portraits of India's Martyrs Drawn in Blood" This act of bravery and patriotism was performed by two great persons from Mathura—Ravi Chandra Gupta and Darshan Singh Vinkal, Retired Vice-principal and an artist respectively. The duo drew portraits of Subhash Chandra Bose and the like, including the soldiers of 1999 Kargil War, with their own blood. Ravi Gupta said these portraits would, in all probability, inculcate in the youth a sense of awareness of the invaluable sacrifices made by national leaders during the freedom struggle against foreign yoke. VHP leader Sadhvi Ritambhara is trying to showcase these artifacts in a museum in Vatsalya gram of Vrindaban near Mathura. However, I suggest that the Government take over these works of art in blood and preserve them for posterity in the National Museum at Delhi. The government should also suitably reward Gupta and Singh who made history by designing our freedom fighters portraits in blood, by their own sacrifices.

❖❖❖

187. BOFORS AS DAMOCLES' SWORD

Bofors demon seems to be hovering over the Congress-led government like a Damocles' sword on a person enjoying a sumptuous feast.

Defreezing of London bank accounts of the Italian businessman Ottavio Quatrocchi, the recipient of the kickbacks in Bofors' 105-mm Howitzer acquisition by the Army and conferring on him a 'clean chit' is a fraud on the nation.

Law Minister H.R. Bhardwaj has committed a grave indiscretion in the matter and he should have resigned as soon as it became public, thanks to the Fourth Estate's vigilance. But, he has not doneso.

Justice in the Bofors' gun deal has been allowed to languish in an 'ad infinitum Q' (Queue) for over two decades. The latest revelation in this case has made a mockery of the Congress-led UPA government's credibility as injustice has been allowed to jump over the queue, riding roughshod over justice in patient waiting.

The Supreme Court's injunction to the Centre to undo the mischief may provide a face-saving device to the government, if it executes it in right earnest.

❖❖❖

188. MORE GENERAL BOGIES NEEDED

The number of general compartments in express and super-fast trains is too small to meet the requirements of the travelling public. At present, only two bogies are provided and they too are overcrowded. Old people, women and children are facing inconvenience as there is hardly any space for them to sit or stand. I myself had gone through the trauma of travelling from Secunderabad to Vijayawada when I boarded a general compartment in East Coast

Express. May I, therefore, request the Railway authorities to increase the number of general compartments in these trains?

❖❖❖

189. PUBLIC SACRIFICE

Sacrifice and service are not uncommon even in these days, when the motto is somehow to make money, legally or illegally, by hook or by crook. In this context, I refer to the news item 'Railway Station by the people'. Four panchayats in Jhunujhunu (Rajasthan) joined hands to build a railway station at Balwantpura with their own resources and labour, as per railway specifications, when the railways expressed their inability to fund the project. Since a few months, the station became operational for travelling public and this contributed more than ₹ 1.5 lakhs to the railway exchequer. This is a shining example of the people's participation in construction, development, growth and improvement of their existing facilities, along with the government's unqualified support. May their tribe increase and thrive.

❖❖❖

190. MINORITY WELFARE

Apropos the editorial 'Armed and Dangerous', it is rightly said that this variant of minority welfare policy can be dangerous, and the next recourse would be separate union budgets for every community. This measure is actually minority warfare against the majority, being pushed through by the so-called secular Congress-led UPA government. Congress governments, successors to British India administration, are following their time-tested divide and rule policy, with an eye on vote bank politics. The British policy imposed separate electorate on British India resulting in its unholy partition in 1947. Successive Congress governments have successfully divided the civil society caste-wise, region-wise and religion-wise. Now, they have laid their hands on the military also. They are implementing a suicidal plan to enumerate the number of Muslims in armed forces which are apolitical and professional. It may be in the interest of the political class but certainly not in national interests.

Such a statistical measure is by no means divisive in its nature, if it is only data collection on Muslim population in the Army for information. But, ulterior motives cannot be ruled out. The government may impose reservations in the Armed forces, which strikes at the root of merit recruitment, prevailing at present in these forces. The venom of separatism is sought to be thrust on the armed forces through back-door methods. It may create segregation on religious lions to the detriment of country's defense capabilities and ever vigilent preparedness.

❖❖❖

191. ADVANTAGE INDIA

In concluding an agreement on civilian nuclear programme on March 2 in New Delhi, both President Bush and Prime Minister Manmohan Singh have carved out a niche for themselves in the annals of diplomatic history. It is a consequence and a consummation of the only agreement between the two in Washington. Mr. Bush was magnanimous enough to accommodate Indian concerns so that India could put its fast-breeder reactor programmes and related research outside the purview of IAEA (International Atomic Energy Agency) safeguards. Now, the onus is on President Bush to get the non-proliferation laws amended in India's favour by the US Congress, where he would be facing rough weather in all probability.

It seems that India is on the threshold of a new vista of attractive opportunities in a new world order dictated by the United States, the sole super-power. The US is indeed keen to tap India's immense expertise and knowledge in various fields including IT. It is also eyeing the 300 million-strong Indian middle class for selling its consumer and capital goods. In addition, they want to sell their military hardware to us. Pentagon's interlocutor is already in New Delhi to clinch a deal for supplying F-16 and F-18 fighter planes against our requirement of Qty 126x combat aircraft, the cost of which runs into billions of dollars. Again, there is also the perceived danger of China emerging as a major economic and military power in the near future, in competition with United States. Befriending India having all the potentialities of a counter-weight to China serves the US policy of balance of power, in the Pacific region. So, the US interests in India are both economic and geo-political. All this is to the advantage of India to gravitate into a major power to play its assigned role in the international arena.

❖❖❖

192. SPEAKER'S ROLE

The first two Speakers G.V. Moulankar and M. Anantasayanam Iyengar of free India upheld the Constitutional norms and conventions without fear or favour in good old days. That was so, in spite of a Prince Charming and a benevolent dictator Jawaharlal Nehru being at the helm of affairs. They neither bent nor crawled before him and never acted according to his whims and fancies. Then came Neelam Sanjiva Reddy during Indira Gandhi's controversial regime. He resigned from the primary membership of the Congress party on being elected as Speaker, to be seen impartial in the discharge of his duties in word and deed and held his head high as Lok Sabha Speaker. In the present Lok Sabha, Speaker Somnath Chatterjee of CPM is setting different standards altogether. Firstly, he could have resigned from his party on becoming Speaker to uphold the impartiality and integrity of the chair but he did not. Secondly, most of his decisions are controversial and intriguing. A case in point is that of the Jharkhand imbroglio over which he covertly disregarded the Supreme Court's directives including summons. Now, in the office of profit episode, he refuses to resign from the post of Speaker saying that his Chairman's post of Sriniketan-Santiniketan Development Authority is not profitable! This comes as an anti-climax to the dramatic resignation of Congress president and UPA chairperson Sonia Gandhi from the 14th Lok Sabha and as Chairperson of the National Advisory Council under duress. Be that as it may, anybody in positions of power has to demonstrate that he is not only 'not corrupt' but should also be seen as above board. Unfortunately, the present Speaker does not qualify this test. This is so, in spite of whatever legislation be made by the Government to save the skin of certain MPs found on the wrong foot holding more than one post of profit.

❖❖❖

193. ZINEDINE ZIDANE STANDS TALL

When the captain of ship is crucified, the vessel becomes rudderless making it vulnerable to sink. This is exactly what has happened to France at the world cup soccer finals at the Olympic stadium in Berlin on July 9. The French captain Zinedine Zidane was ousted from the field during the dying minutes of the game for head-butting the Italian defender Marco Materazzi must have demoralised Les Bleus the French team as a whole. With this unexpected advantage, the Azzuris romped home with a 5-3 victory against France. I feel that, in this case, the culprit was Marco Materazzi who subjected Zidane to verbal abuse of his family members more than twice. To get emotional rage over such an indecent behaviour on the playground is natural and Zidane did just that, pinning his opponent to the ground. Matarazzi used his tactics of insult to get the redoubtable Zidane out of play and it worked well. Be it as it may, Zidane stands tall in this game alongside the best players of the world like Pele, Diego Maradona, Ronaldo and Ronaldinho. Deservedly, he was awarded "Golden Ball for the Best Player" by the Journalists.

❖❖❖

194. FILE NOTINGS

The editorial 'File it, Forget it' on UPA Government's decision to exclude official file notings from the purview of RTI (Right to information) Act is intriguing. It speaks of subversion of our right to information. As a person who worked in the Union Government departments in various capacities for over 25 years, I will broadly differ with this assertion. There is a definitive set procedure followed in the Government before finalising a decision on any matter. Every official has his own ideas on any subject coming up for his comments or opinion and he accordingly puts them in writing in the concerned file for consideration of his immediate superior. In turn, his superior sends the file with remarks, if any, to the next higher official and the file moves on and on to reach the decision-making desk.

Thus, decisions are arrived at, based on technical details and inputs provided at every level of governmental hierarchy. Now, all these recordings are strictly confidential and internal and outsiders need not worry about them. It is a moot point whether a commoner/*aam admi* is interested in such official notings on file but for the decision taken thereupon which may have a direct bearing on his life's parameters. A knowledge of official notings is of little use for any agency other than the government, except for harassing or witch-hunting of the officials involved. And so, RTI Act should allow access to the final outcome but not to related minutes or notes. The Government is perfectly right in bestowing indemnity to its officialdom in expressing their views in the file notings without fear or favour of being publicised.

❖❖❖

195. SALAAM MUMBAIKARS

Mumbaikars' resilience in the quick recovery from the shock and terror of serial bomb blast massacre on July 11 in their city within a matter of 12 hours, in the face of an amazing static inaction of the ruling clique, is commendable. This typical character of Mumbaikars is worth emulating in other parts of the country when such gory incidents occur at irregular intervals, as witnessed for the last 15 years. All the same, our Government's response to the crime of killing innocent civilians is woefully appalling and ludicrous. With usual refrain, they say, "We will not be cowed down in our persistent pursuit of peace with Pakistan" inspite of terrorist violence in Indian Kashmir and prominent cities like Ahmedabad, Bangalore, Delhi, Mumbai and Varanasi. They shield their political impotency and non-performance by brave rhetoric, unmindful of deaths and destruction perpetrated by violent acts sponsored across the border.

In this context, Pakistan Foreign Minister Khurshid Mahmood Kasuri's observations portend ominous consequences for both the countries. It spells a fortuitous warning that unless the Kashmir issue is solved to the satisfaction of Pakistan, India will not be allowed to surge ahead with peace and prosperity. It entails the mandarins of South Block to resurvey the whole gamut of Pakistan's intransigent attitude towards India, since the unholy partition in 1947, claiming in its wake enormous casualties terms of life and property, in its wake. India has bled for long. 'Thus far and no further'. Let the government show its resolve to crush internal terrorism of all types, either sponsored or home-made. It should realise that Pakistan could come to terms with India if and only we pay them in their own coin by supporting freedom fighters of Balochistan.

❖❖❖

196. UNWARRANTED MOVE

The editorial 'More Arab than Arabs' seems to bestow the benefit of doubt on the UPA Government while castigating the Leftists for their indefensible stance on Israel. I hold no brief for the Leftist outfits. Still, it is a moot point whether the UPA Government would have acted differently. Where is the need for UPA helmsmen to get a resolution passed by Lok Sabha condemning Israel for its indiscriminate bombing of Lebanon when even its neighbours like Syria and Jordan are keeping a low profile? Instead, a statement seeking cessation of hostilities would have been enough. And so, it is rightly said, 'Fools rush in where the angels fear to tread'. Israel's punitive action against the terrorist organisation Hizbollah and its hideouts in Lebanon is being viewed positively by many non-committal Indians, particularly because the UPA Government dithered inexplicably, in the aftermath of terrorist outfits Lakshar-e-Toiba and SIMI's serial bomb blasts in Mumbai. Israel is appreciated for its steely determination to root out terrorists. In contrast, it is felt that UPA and Leftists are hand-in-glove to be passive spectators to the tragedy that befalls commoners due to terrorism.

❖❖❖

197. TELANGANA GIMMICKRY

After going through 58 days of gruelling ordeal of fast, Potti Sriramulu succumbed to inevitable death on 15th Dec., 1952, for the formation of Andhra State with Madras as capital, by bifurcating the then composite Madras presidency. However, Andhra state was formed only on 1 Oct., 1954 with Andhra Kesari Tanguturi Prakasam as Chief Minister and Kurnool as capital instead of Madras. In contrast, very recently, TRS supremo Kalwakurthy Chandrasekhar Rao fasted barely for two days for achieving the Telangana state, waiting with bated breath for over six hours for the arrival of Union

Minister Sharad Pawar to conclude his fast. Would the T-state be formed with such gimmickry?

❖❖❖

198. HUMOUR AT BEST

I appreciate the sense of humour and sarcasm in the editorial 'People for Pluto'. It makes light of International Astronomical Union's (IAU's) decision to demote Pluto from its planetary status. Its existence, however, is not called into question and is given its due as an astronomical object along with Charon and Xena (1B03£313), the trio being named Plutons. Again, together with Ceres, these foursome are called Dwarf Planets. Thus, though no more a planet revolving in an elliptical orbit with Sun as one of its foci, it still retains its planetary position as a Dwarf. And so, there may be no need for Indian propensity to go in for a PIL in Supreme Court or American proclivity to consider moving a Security Council resolution, as Pluto is named after American who discovered it in 1930. It is interesting to note in this regard that Indian astrologers never consider Pluto as a planet (Graham) in their calculations for predicting the future of people.

❖❖❖

199. HELP BALOCH PEOPLE

The Balochistan problem has remained unsolved since its forced merger with Pakistan in steps, with British connivance – first Quetta region under British in 1947 and then tribal states under Khan of Kalat in 1948. It constituted more than half the area of Pakistan, bordering Afghanistan and Baloch region of Iran. It is also an unfinished agenda of partition, just like Kashmir as per Pakistan's perspective. Now, the tragic killing of tribal patriarch Nawab Akbar Khan Bugti in his own hideout far from Quetta, by the Pakistan Army on August 26, has led to an upheaval of simmering discontent among Baloch nationalists. India should not be a silent spectator to whatever happens in its neighbourhood. It must render material help to Baloch people in their hour of trial, not fully but substantially, without fear or favour, to atone for its errors of judgment during partition.

❖❖❖

200. MODERN 'TULA RANAM'

In the days of yore, if there were two contesting princes for the throne of a kingdom, a fight was arranged between the two and the winner was awarded the throne. This was called 'Tula Ranam' (War between equals) in which only the contestants fight while all others are spectators. Jarasandh, the King of Magadh (the present-day Bihar) was killed by Bhimasen, the Pandava Prince in such a mutual fight.

In the epic Mahabharat, a 'Tula Ranam' would have occurred between Karna, the trusted lieutenant of Kourava Prince Duryodhana and Arjun, the Pandava Prince, had Duryodhan agreed to the suggestion of Bhishma Pitamaha and Guru Dronacharya. The subsequent 18-day war, which led to the decimation of Kouravas except Yuyuthsa, who shifted his allegiance to Pandavas, is common knowledge.

Now, the modern 'Tula Ranam' (electoral battle) to occur between Sports Minister M. Satyanarayana Rao and TRS chief K. Chandrasekhara Rao for Karimnagar Parliamentary Constituency on Telangana issue has been nipped in the bud in the green room by the Congress High Command to the detriment of itself. The Congress seems to be intent on commiting "Hara-Kiri" in Telangana through its un imaginative acts.

❖❖❖

201. EXHILARATING

Pieces of inquisitive knowledge are contained in the news item 'World Ramayana Meet in Romania'. It is exhilarating to note that a far-away East European country Romania has about 8000 Romani words which are derivatives of Hindi and Sanskrit vocabulary. It is also a revelation to most of the discerning Indians that this country is inhabited by a majority of European gypsies who claim their ancestry to India. Its capital Bucharest on the banks of a tributary to river Danube, possesses an Indian library within the Romanian national library complex.

The crux of the news is that it will be hosting the 23rd international Ramayana conference, the earlier one having been held in Birmingham, Britain. It is a matter of deep appreciation for us that this epic is popular not only in Indonesia's Bali Island in Pacific Ocean but in some European countries as well, like Romania.

❖❖❖

202. INDIAN ARMY

The Indian Armed forces have gained considerable experience and expertise in critical fields like security and strategy having successfully handled diversified conflict situations in the form of external aggression and internal insurgency. Thus, these domains are more a preserve of military than bureaucrcy. And the military participation is absolutely essential in security and strategic planning. In this context, I appreciate and commend the article 'Why exclude Army from security-think' by former VCOAS (Vice-chief of Army Staff) Lt. Gen. Vijay Oberoi. It puts the security syndrome of our country in its proper perspective.

Conducting deliberations of NSC (National Security Council) and its ancillaries NSAB (Nation Security Advisory Board) and SPG (Strategic Policy Group) without substantial military participation is like enacting the Shakespearean drama 'Hamlet' without the Prince of Denmark. At present, these security groupings have meagre military presence. But, military inputs are necessary ingredients in any strategic policy formulation, particularly with regard to our neighbours China and Pakistan. And to marginalise senior military personnel from decision-making processes is detrimental to our national interests. Hence, the Central Government should have a second look at the composition of national security groupings to accommodate Armed forces personnel of higher echelons.

❖❖❖

203. AMUSING

On reading the news item "ICC's Not East India Company", I was infinitely amused that East India Company of yore has figured in the tussle between BCCI and ICC over 'Membership Participation Agreement (MPA)' and in particular over BCCI's selection of Mohammed Azharuddin (the celebrated Indian cricketer who had been implicated and indicted in 'match fixing' episode), for felicitation.

East India Company of Britian came to India in the beginning of the 17th century for trade but engaged itself in empire building thus conquering India as a jewel in the British crown. But ICC can, in no way, win over BCCI, even in its wildest dreams.

Such comparisons are odious. It is not very flattering for BCCI official Lalit Modi to compare ICC which represents the world cricket having 97 cricketing countries including India as its members with East India Company. To put unlikely elements in juxtaposition is no act of wisdom and should better, be avoided. However, ICC chief Malcolm Speed made a heartening gesture saying that they are not against Azharuddin being honoured by BCCI.

❖❖❖

204. ALWAYS PASSIVE

The euphoria generated in certain sections of the fourth estate and the government during Chinese President Hu Jintao's four-day visit to India is not correlated but divorced from ground realities. We are not worried to get back the vast areas of Aksai Chin occupied by China during its 1962 aggression. Neither are we worried about the areas of Pakistan-occupied Kashmir including Gilgit gifted to China by Pakistan. But, unlike us, the Chinese claim the whole of Arunachal Pradesh without compunction and dispute the Mc-Mohan line boundary between India and Tibet. Yes! Tibet, because we have no border with China before they occupied Tibet during 1950s. And we preferred to be onlookers turning a Nelson's eye, as Tibet lost its buffer-state status between us and China. This is Pandit Nehru's grievous fault, though he was shrewd enough to admit that while we can deal with Russia in peace, the same cannot be said of China.

Actually, China made progressive geography when we were making rueful history of sorts.

True, we are always the aggrieved and not the aggressor throughout our cheque red history. Our policy so far had been – "when you are attacked, you defend; if you cannot, you surrender to the enemy." But, this has resulted in disastrous consequences for us. Even now, after almost 60 years of independence, we are oblivious to the intrigues of our inimical neighbours. We only respond to their overtures without any shrewd initiatives on our part.

❖❖❖

205. TOO RARE

Mahatma Gandhi has introduced the moral element in Indian polity. Over the years, it progressively deteriorated and became a rare commodity. At present, it has become almost extinct. The Shibu Soren episode proves the same, if proof is required. He relinquished his office only at the Prime Minister's insistence, even after he was found guilty by a Delhi court, in the extermination of his private secretary Sashinath Jha. And now, the court sentenced him to life imprisonment on the same count. But, still he found it prudent to retain his parliamentary membership. His is not an isolated case. There are many skeletons like him in the cupboards of both the UPA and NDA. And they are at fault to keep undesirable persons in their fold thus maligning India's democratic parliamenary system. Another Gandhi may not arrive on the scene, for 'moral rearmament' of these political entities. Only a quirk of fate can save the country from such coalition conglomerations.

❖❖❖

206. THOUGHT-PROVOKING

The editorial 'History and Our Story' is thought-provoking, though I differ with it in details. True. There is no love lost between Balochistan and NWFP leaders and Mohammed Ali Jinnah since pre-partition days. Even so, I consider that JUI (Jamait Ulema-e-Islam) Chief Moulana Fazlur Rehman's remarks that Jinnah had done nothing worth-remembering to be honoured as freedom fighter, are honest and unbiased. Yes. He led an aristocratic life and made no sacrifice to achieve freedom of the Indian sub-continent.

And present standards, which are devoid of morality, may still be applied to retell the past history and its heroes, provided facts are not twisted and moulded to suit the present circumstances, as these are different from those of the past.

None can deny the fact that the lives of Gandhi, Nehru, Patel, Subhash Bose and Frontier Gandhi (Khan Abbdul Gaffar Khan) are sagas of sacrifice and suffering. Again, USA would not have been a superpower, had not President Abraham Lincoln saved it from disintegration, risking a civil war in 19th century. Also, there is no denying that Richard Nixon had the vision of an emerging China from its dark ages, to make up with it. In other words, I would say that story-writing about past heroes should be factual and objective as history is but the story of such heroes and their heroic deeds.

❖❖❖

207. JOB QUOTA

UP Chief Minister Mayawati's 30 per cent job reservation formula in exchange for quite a few substantial financial props from the government for private sector industrial concerns and educational institutions both existing and those to be established, is innovative and commendable. This 30 per cent quota consists of 10 per cent for SC, 10 per cent for OBC and 10 per cent for economically backward upper castes. Over and above, it would be a voluntary arrangement. Those who want state's financial support should implement the said proposals *in toto* and those who do not want the same, would be under no compulsion to implement 30 per cent job quota.

UPA Government's HRD Ministry under Arjun Singh may take a leaf-out of Mayawati's imaginative formula and go in for voluntary adoption of their 27 per cent OBC quota in both public and private enterprises including institutions of higher learning like IIMs, IITs and AIIMS. It should, however, be borne in mind that these reservations could not be continued indefinitely, *ad infinitum*. At some defining point of time, they have got to be discontinued counting only on merit, if India were to shine in the comity of nations by virtue of its intellectual property.

❖❖❖

208. GODSE STATUE

I refer to the news item "Tension as Gandhians, Foil VHP Move to Unveil Godse Statue" feel that both the parties involved in the incident are at fault. Shyam Prasad Mukherjee, a prominent lawyer of Tadepalligudem built a statue of Godse in his backyard without seeking permission of any competent authority – either court or police. So it is, no doubt, an ill-conceived task at variance with people's sentiments. He obviously knows it and performed the same, may be, to get cheap popularity. The violent action by noted, Gandhian Pratti Seshaiah, assisted by a few members of Gandhian societies, in destroying the statue by entering the premises of the advocate is un-Gandhian and unlawful. It is against all decent norms and Gandhian principles of non-violence and non-cooperation. They could have easily brought the police into picture, before they destroyed the statue. Instead, they brought the demolition-remnants to police custody, with a complaint as well! By their quixotic act, they did incalculable disservice to Mahatma Gandhi and his noble doctrines. Perhaps, this is the trend of 21st century Gandhians.

❖❖❖

209. MANY DOUBTS OVER COOPERATIVE FARMING

In response to the State government's plans to implement cooperative farming, I would like to state that it was only partially successful even in Communist countries like China and the erstwhile Soviet Union, where coercive methods were used. 'Cooperative culture' in any field has not been fully successful, as in the case of urban cooperative banks. Moreover, it is impossible for farmers to surrender their legal ownership rights on their land holdings to a cooperative society, except under coercion, as their emotional attachment to the land is deep-rooted. The existing problems of farming community are due to shortage of agricultural implements like fertilizers and intermittent power supply.

If these are supplied to meet the demands of the farmers, then output per acre would multiply substantially. It will be prudent to take up the pilot project of cooperative farming in select villages only after carrying out a feasibility study.

❖❖❖

210. DISCUSS PRESSING PROBLEMS

The mutual recriminations between Chief Minister Y.S. Rajasekhara Reddy and the leader of the Opposition N. Chandrababu Naidu on a regular basis in the Legislative Assembly is causing consternation among the public. Instead of attending to pressing problems like severe drought conditions and the sky-rocketing prices of essential commodities that are affecting the poor and the middle class, they revel in their spats. This is unpardonable waste of Assembly time and taxpayers' hard earned money used to keep the Assembly sessions going on. Both the feuding leaders are requested to use the Assembly sessions to discuss public problems and find out solutions to them.

❖❖❖

211. TIME TO MITIGATE FARMER'S TRAVAILS

Monsoon has failed, and there are no seasonal rains so far in the State. In particular, there is a scanty rainfall in Godavari and Krishna deltas which are considered to be granaries of the State. The riverbeds themselves have become parched in many parts. Large tracts of agricultural land may go dry if this anomalous dry spell continues for another two months, when the rainy season ends. The resultant drought situation could, indeed, prove to be grave. In fact, drought conditions already exist in over 900 mandals as per unofficial estimates. Even so, the government seems to be oblivious to the intensity of the crisis, as it did not initiate any contingency plan to mitigate the toiling farmers' travails. At least now, the government should take remedial measures like granting of a minimum compensation of ₹ 5,000 per acre to the farmers who lost their crops and providing of 50 kg of rice to the families of agricultural labourers.

❖❖❖

212. JASWANT'S EXPULSION

Apropos the news item "Jinnah Demonized by India", says Jaswant Singh let me say, it is all a phantasmagoria of horrible nonsense. I am old enough to recall that it was Mohammad Ali Jinnah who formulated his pernicious "Two-Nation Theory" for Muslims and Hindus, in 1940. He initiated "Direct Action" on 16th August, 1946 to achieve Pakistan, a homeland for Muslims with Muslim majority provinces. It resulted in the "Great Communal Carnage" in Calcutta and elsewhere. In fact, he served as "Crescent card" of the British to partition India, as an extension of their "Divide and Rule" Policy. The circumstances had so cropped up during 1946-47 that division of the sub-continent on religious basis became inescapable. And the role of Jinnah was indeed substantial in the 'cataclysmic event'. He was the messiah of Pakistan and could not be a "Great Indian demonized".

❖❖❖

213. INCISIVE ARTICLE

Aditya Sinha's article "Mewing Tiger, Roaring Dragon" is incisive, forthright and logical. Instead of roaring, the tiger mews while the dragon roars instead of hissing. Indian policy for China or Pakistan is weak-kneed. The Hindi-Chini Bhai-Bhai policy of Jawaharlal Nehru resulted in Indo-Chinese war of 1962. China has indeed taught a lesson to India that China counts in Asia and world at large and not India. But we refuse to learn from history and come to grief invariably. Since the Communist takeover in 1949, China marched its People's Liberation Army to annex Turkestan/Xinjiang and Tibet in quick succession. Now, they say Arunachal Pradesh is Chinese territory calling it lower/south Tibet. India can be sure that the Chinese hegemonic demands will not end with Arunachal Pradesh. It may turn a Nelson's eye to ground realities to its own discomfiture.

❖❖❖

214. HYDERABAD AS CAPITAL

As an 80-year-old, I recall Fazl Ali Commission's recommendations for the formation of Telangana State. Further, Telangana was merged with Andhra State and Andhra Pradesh formed with capital in Hyderabad on the insistence of a respected

Congress leader from Telangana, Burgula Ramakrishna Rao. Since then, both the regions have become uneasy bed-fellows (and the people and leaders of both the regions were responsible for the separatist movements in 1969 (Telangana) and 1973 (Jai Andhra). Now, TRS Chief K. Chandrasekhara Rao's indefinite fast since November 29, has not only whipped up emotions among student community, government employees and the so-called intellectuals of the region, but also led to unabated vandalism.

These days even age-old joint families are splitting up as they are no longer able to continue to live with harmony. And so it would be better if the Andhra Pradesh is bifurcated without delay and Hyderabad made the common capital for both the States, for a few years.

❖❖❖

215. TELANGANA ISSUE

The die is cast for the formation of Telangana state due to emotional black-mail of elector rejected T.R.S. Chief K. Chandrasekhara Rao's 11-day indefinite-fast (!) and unmitigated violence in that region. He was doubly successful in forcing the government to accept his separatist demand and uniting Telangana legislators of all hues to unequivocally support separation. It is now too late to agitate for united Andhra Pradesh by hunger strikes and violent agitations. Though unprecedented in the legislative history of free India, the resignations of over 135 MLAs of Andhra and Rayalaseema irrespective of party affiliations is un-warranted and futile. It is also black-mail. Better they impress Congress hierarchy for trifurcation so that the coastal region may develop unhindered, without being saddled by another agitation for Rayalaseema. You can't keep unwilling partners with you.

❖❖❖

216. UNFULFILLED QUEST

The editorial "Unfulfilled Quest" on BJP Leader Lal Krishna Advani's political career spanning over seven decades was factual and logical. I would say that Mr. Advani's fall in the BJP began with his "Jinnah-was-secular" speech in Pakistan. He fell out of favour with the RSS. Even at 82, a Swayamsevak since the age of 15, he would have remained the leading light of the BJP but for the RSS insistence on a generational change. "Old order changes yielding place to new" as enunciated by the famous poet Lord Tennyson. But, there is no guarantee that the young will be more efficient and politically wise. The BJP is unlikely to become a viable Opposition unless it frees itself from the RSS stranglehold.

❖❖❖

217. CHECK PRICE RISE

The MLAs are said to be people's representatives. They take the people for granted after getting elected. They attribute their political agitations to the people's will and wish and say these are carried out by the people, for the people and of the people. In the preceding agitations for bifurcation of the State, and united Andhra, there is little or no people's participation. People are not worried whether they will be in AP or Telangana. All they want is control of the astronomical rise in prices of essential commodities by the government of the day.

❖❖❖

218. GREAT LEADER

Jyoti Basu, a Bar-at-law brought respectability to the communist movement in India. He was the unquestioned leader of CPM since its birth 1964. During his uninterrupted 23-year Chief Ministership, he reformed and transformed West Bengal into a well-governed model state for others to emulate including the Congress ruled ones. He was a gentleman or Bhadrapurush in the crop of unprincipled and unscrupulous political pigmies. Though wedded to communism, he was a democrat in equal measure, next only to Jawaharlal Nehru. In his passing a way, CPM has lost a charismatic leader. At least now, the Union Government should honour him with "Bharat Ratna", posthumously, since he was a great leader among the Indian communists.

❖❖❖

219. RECOVER PROPERTY LOSS FROM POLITICAL PARTIES

The Andhra Pradesh State Road Transport Corporation (APSRTC) has increased the bus fares substantially. The authorities have quoted periodic increase in the prices of fuel, spare parts and tyres as the reason for the fare hike, which is unexceptionable. The unannounced reason, however, is the burning of over 600 buses by the activists during the movements for separate Telangana and unified Andhra Pradesh. Instead of extracting the monetary losses incurred therein from the commuters by hiking the bus fares, the authorities should make good the same from the political parties responsible for the wanton destruction. The government must amend the Criminal Procedure Code laws to this effect.

❖❖❖

220. RAJPAKSA'S VICTORY

Sri Lankan President Mahinda Rajapaksa's greatest contribution to the Island nation is "PEACE", by the elimination of a declared terrorist organization LTTE's violent activities hanging fire for over three decades, through relentless military action. This peace should not be the peace of the grave-yard. Now that he has won a thumping victory for a second presidential term over the combined opposition candidate Gen. Sarath Fonseka (Retd), he should direct all his energies to achieve permanent peace by solving the issues pestering the ethnic Tamil minority in the north, by devolution of certain essential powers to them so that they feel they are equal citizens to their Buddhist counterparts in the south.

❖❖❖

221. INFLATION

As per the indicators of growth and inflation projected by the government agencies, the GDP would be 7.75 per cent to 7.9 per cent, for the current financial year 2010-11. The inflation rates may reach an all-time high with the contemplated increase in the prices of petroleum products. Going by the present situation, one can assume that the inflation rates in the near future would be increased further. In such a situation, the plight of common man can be easily imagined. So far, both the State and Centre did nothing to bring down prices of essential commodities. They must initiate suitable measures to control the price spiral to elleviate the plight of the commoners and poor.

❖❖❖

222. NEW LOOK TEAM

The BJP under Nitin Gadkari made a judicious choice of man and women of experience and youth for its organizational set-up. It has stolen a march over other parties by giving 33 per cent representation to women in party posts. The selection of Najma Heptullah and Mukhtar Abbas Naqvi as Vice-presidents, however, will cut no ice with the Muslim community, as simultaneously the stormy-petral Varun Gandhi has been made Secretary. When all is said and done, the BJP can become acceptable to the secular people of India only when it breaks free of the stranglehold of its mentor RSS.

❖❖❖

223. WHOSE LOSS?

Professor Dhirendra Sharma's account ("It was I who lost, not Gandhiji,") portrays free India's politicians in their true colours. Men like Prof. Sharma who had the courage of conviction to reject a politician's urge to incite violence are rare to come by now. Being an octogenarian, I can vouchsafe that Mahatma Gandhi's non-violent, non-cooperation agitations in 1920 and 1930 and the quit India movement in 1942 invariably led to violence. But then we were fighting against a colonial government for our Independence. Now, it is our own democratically elected government. Even so, it has become customary for people and their leaders to drift into violence to highlight their grievances, attributing it to Gandhian methods. In a democracy, there is no need for violent agitations and intimidating fasts to press for and achieve any demand. People's representatives can make the government concede the legitimate demands through discussion and debate.

❖❖❖

224. UNPOPULAR MEASURE

The Central Government recently hiked the prices of petrol and diesel, which would, in turn, push up the already spiraling prices of essential commodities. The decontrolling of price regime only benefits oil firms. They would periodically increase the fuel oil prices and for every increase, there would be a corresponding increase in prices of essential commodities. This would lead to a continuous shrinkage in the real incomes of the poor and the lower middle class. Obviously, the government is intent on protecting the health of its fiscal management and that of the oil companies. The reasons for these unpopular measures are that the government thinks the upper middle class (the new rich) and the old rich are not unduly worried about inflationary trends, political opposition is in a disarray and the general elections are a good four years away.

❖❖❖

225. DANGEROUS INDEED

The editorial "Mamata's Dangerous Game" is a critical comment on the government's contradictory position in allowing the Railway Minister Mamata Banerjee to hobnob with armed Maoist insurgents, with whom the para-military forces are engaged in armed struggle. She should not be allowed to indulge such indiscretions anymore. The government seems to be a prisoner of indecision in dealing with either errant ministers or the canker of Maoism. When the Prime Minister Manmohan Singh declared that Maoists are the greatest internal security threat to the country, it is incumbent on him to follow it up in right earnest with complementary counterinsurgency operations both by military and civil agencies; the former to clear Maoist infested regions and the latter to build administrative, economic and social infrastructure in those liberated areas. In addition, his cabinet should also be cleared of elements like Mamata Didi, who sympathies with Maoists for their own selfish motives. Any prevarication or any other course of action in this regard would be detrimental to national interests. However, the present inaction of the government on this score may lead to unforeseen circumstances from which it would be difficult to emerge unscathed.

❖❖❖

226. MP'S ALLOWANCES

Members of Parliament recently voted in favour of a three-fold increase in their salaries and simultaneously doubling of their constituency and office expense allowances along with daily sitting allowances. The government seems to be happy to pilot the concerned money bill. This was done at a time when millions of countrymen are being weighed down by financial burden due to the unmitigated inflation and ever-increasing price spiral of essential commodities.

The unseemly haste the Government has shown to hike MP's salaries is surprising, while it overlooked the long pending demand of ex-servicemen seeking one rank, one pension (OROP) which would benefit them monetarily; they did yeoman service to defend the country's borders. Common people feel that there is absolutely no immediacy for hiking MP's pay packets, as they freely enjoy innumerable perks and have various sources of income known and unknown. They also enjoy lavish style of living, what with free air and rail travel, free medical treatment in India and/or abroad and free accommodation in Lutyens' New Delhi. Even so, they wanted an unjustified increase in their emoluments, without caring for public resentment. There is growing cynicism about the political class as a whole among the discerning public.

❖❖❖

227. CHANGE IN AP

The well-balanced editorial "Volatile Andhra Pradesh" unequivocally puts the fluid situation in AP in its right perspective. Also, the corresponding "Cartoonscape" is a fitting analogy between "the changeover of older Rosaiah (78) to the younger N. Kiran Kumar Reddy (50)" and the game of Cricket. All the same, it is beyond my comprehension that Rosaiah had to resign only due to his old age and his disinclination to discipline Y.S. Jagan Mohan Reddy and his antics. Even the Congress High Command is prisoner of indecision in the latter's case. Instead of taking stern action against Jagan, it has opted for a change of chief minister, making Rosaiah a scapegoat in the process. Even now it has to advise the new Chief Minister to take control of the emerging situation and put Jagan in his place, as any Congress chief minister acts only on the instructions of the High Command.

❖❖❖

228. LOOKING AT HISTORY

This is with respect to the article "From the Ashes of Empire" by former Lt. Gen. S.K. Sinha. I am an avid reader of the General's articles. As an octogenarian, I get excited to recapitulate the cataclysmic events of those momentous days, thanks to the General. Indeed, Dec. 7, 1941, the day of decimation of US Eastern Fleet in PEARL HARBOUR by Japanese Naval Command, rang the death-knell of the Imperialist forces in south and south-east Asian countries. I recall this historic day with justifiable pride, as I was the first to inform my Vakil father, the news of Japanese attack on Pearl Harbour, having heard the same in the early hours in our home town Gudivada (Dist. Krishna) on the very same day. I appreciate Deccan Chronicle for publishing the General's first-hand account of that almost forgotten era.

❖❖❖

229. JPC PROBE

The editorial "Offence as Defence" gives a clear and logical perspective of the multi-crore 2G Spectrum allocation scam. Sonia Gandhi taking umbrage under a military dictum would not put the scam under wraps, even as a combined opposition would not be cowed down by such tactics. The principle of collective/joint responsibility of cabinet system puts the onus on prime minister to initiate suitable action on the mater. The UPA Government under him could have easily accepted the opposition demand for a JPC probe. The Government's obstinacy in not going for JPC and opposition's obduracy in stalling parliament proceedings for more than two weeks is not in the interests of tax payer money. Perhaps, the government is fearing that more skeletons in its cupboard would come under public scrutiny. Be it as it may, the government cannot escape accountability by dangling 'Damocles' Sword' of mid-term poll on the opposition. It would do well to remember that former Prime Minister Mrs. Indira Gandhi met her Waterloo in 1977 general elections by a determined opposition of warring parties named Janata. After all, it is answerable to the common people and tax payers who bear the albatross burden of government's financial irregularities.

❖❖❖

230. DEMOCRATIC WAY OUT

Former Supreme Court Judge Justice Sri Krishna, Chairman of the committee formed to look into the demand for separate Telangana or unified Andhra Pradesh, recently stated in Hyderabad that his judgement may please some sections and displeased others.

"But accepting judgements that displeases us is the essence of democracy", he said. This is the cardinal principal to be followed by all the political parties who swear by democratic norms. Constitution allows only for peaceful methods and agitations. All the leaders would be advised to heed and honour the sane advice of Sri Krishna Committee and follow peaceful methods to highlight their grievances, if any. Any political party or person should not instigate and round the passions of students and their party cadre to perpetrating violent acts resulting in the damage and destruction of public and private properties, after the report is made public.

❖❖❖

231. EGYPTIAN UNREST

The editorial "Egypt Shakes West Asia" and the article "Egypt: How India Should Respond?" by Chinmaya R. Gharekhan put the Egyptian imbroglio in the correct perspective. The uprising seems to be spontaneous what with people of every walk of live joining it. Egypt has a long history of oppression under strong military leaders like Gamal Abdel Naser, Anwar El Sadat and Hosni Mubarak; though they are all celebrated secular stalwarts and India's friends. Poverty, sky-rocketing food prices and unemployment which were not attended to by successive governments are obviously the immediate reason for the present turmoil. President Mubarak now at 82, had 30-year long innings in power and should step down in favour of either Gen. Omar Soleiman. His Vice-President or Mohammed el Baradei former Chairman of UN Nuclear Agency. Procrastination could result in the ascension of fundamentalist

Muslim Brotherhood headed by Mohammed Badie/Mohammed Mursi to power. As India has good relations with Egypt since Naser's time, it would be prudent, in its own interest, to support any regime that comes to power, as it did with Myanmar's Military Government. It should not interfere in the ongoing peoples' movement to export democracy.

❖❖❖

232. MODI'S ICON; SARDAR PATEL

Apropos the editorial "Rediscovering Patel" and various earlier letters on Narendra Modi's factual assertions on Patel, let me say that Modi is not far off the truth. Few like me in their 80s would recall that Sardar Vallabhbhai Jhaverbhai Patel would have easily become the first Prime Minister of India, as 7 out of 11 British Indian provinces opted for him. But Mahatma Gandhi, the then High Command vetoed it and anointed Pandit Jawaharlal Nehru for the top job. Patel, as a true Gandhian, agreed to work under Panditji. Nehru was a visionary and utopian while Patel was a realistic and practical down-to-earth man. There are bound to be differences of opinion between the two. But, they were not insurmountable and they respected each other. In one or two occasions, Gandhi had to seek the good officers of Lord Lewis Mountbatten, the then Governor-General to mediate between the two stalwarts.

Now, as Congressmen have almost forgotten Patel's contribution in merging 560 and odd princely states into Indian union, in their misplaced zeal of sycophancy of Nehru's descendants so far, I find nothing wrong if BJP or its PM candidate Modi try to eulogize Patel as Bismarck of India and also construct "a statue of unity" in commemoration of Sardar Patel. It could be for political dividends, no doubt. But, are Congress leaders any different, who cultivate commoners by offering loaves and fishes on the eve of coming general elections?

❖❖❖